LAY-LED LITURGIES
for PROPHETIC TIMES

WILLIAM J. BAUSCH

Published by:

Clear Faith Publishing
781 Caxambas Drive
Marco Island, FL 34145

Unless otherwise stated, William J. Bausch uses his own trans-
lation and/or paraphrase of scripture. For this work, Father Bill
drew primarily from the New American Bible, revised edition
and the *Lectionary for Mass for Use in the Dioceses of the
United States of America, second typical edition.*

Official Mass prayers are from the *Lectionary for Mass for Use
in the Dioceses of the United States of America, second typical
edition,* Copyright 1970, 1986, 1997, 1998, 2001, Confraternity of
Christian Doctrine, Inc. The official Sacrament and other rituals
are to be found in *The Rites of the Catholic Church,* Liturgical
Press, 1990.

Clip art by Steve Erspamer, Liturgy Training Publications,
Archdiocese of Chicago.

ISBN: 978-1-940414-34-8
Cover & Interior Design by Doug Cordes

The mission of Clear Faith Publishing is to spread joy, peace,
and comfort through great writing about spirituality, religion,
and faith that touches the reader and serves those who live
on the margins. Portions of the proceeds from this book are
donated to organizations that feed, shelter, and provide counsel
for those in need.

For more information, please visit us at:
www.clearfaithpublishing.com.

Gaudeamus igitur,

Juvenes dum sumus.

Post iucundam iuventutem,

Post molestam senectutem,

Nos habebit humus.

In memoriam

ROCCO CUOMO

Priest and Friend

TABLE OF CONTENTS

ACKNOWLEDGMENTS

I wish to thank my publisher, Jim Knipper, for his faith in and support of this book; Shirin McArthur for her expert editing in finding sources and rescuing errant commas, bad spelling, and some incoherent sentences; Rev. Michael Hall, director of the liturgical commission of the Diocese of Trenton for his help; Wanda Garrin, Engaged Living Coordinator at the Apple-wood senior residence where I live, for her assistance in helping me prepare these liturgies for the residents; and Angela Kinlin and her friends from my former parish, who ferreted out the half-century-old original booklets of some of these liturgies.

The INTRODUCTIONS

ℐ MUST-READ INTRODUCTION

Let me begin by relating how I came to write this book, for it explains what it is all about. About six years ago, I contracted a deadly sepsis virus that nearly killed me. Unable to care for myself, I moved to a secular senior residence. Slowly recovering from the sepsis and later achieving remission from acute leukemia, I was eventually able to care for myself. The Roman Catholics at the residence, like those of other denominations, were bused to the local parish for Sundays and special feast days. Then, some five years later, the COVID-19 pandemic of 2020–2021 hit and we, being the vulnerable cohort, were severely quarantined. We were all in virtual lockdown for over a year.

For the first time in their lives, my fellow Catholics had to forego their dearly cherished religious practices. No Mass, ashes, palms, Advent wreath blessing, days of recollection. No Christmas Mass, Holy Thursday, Good Friday, Stations of the Cross, Easter. No Easter Duty confession, Novenas, Benediction, and so on. The mental health burdens of confinement and isolation were bad enough. Not having the comfort of their religion was devastating.

It would have been a spiritual-mental disaster—except, by accident (or God's design?), I was here. So, I wrote liturgies for them, covering the feasts and devotions you see in the Table of Contents. I added speaking parts, ran off copies, and stapled them together so that each had his or her own "missalette." This book—or perhaps "manual" might be a better description—is the result. *When I pass on, they can still worship.* They have the tools—and that's my point: Lay-led leadership will save the day.

Then I thought: What about all those *other* senior residences and nursing homes that are sprouting like mushrooms? Approximately ten thousand people turn 65 every day,[1] and 16.6

. . . .

1 United Nations Population Division, as quoted in American Association of Retired Persons, *The Aging Readiness & Competitiveness Report*, https://arc.aarpinternational.org/File%20Library/Full%20Reports/ARC-Report---United-States.pdf.

percent of the US population is currently 65 or older.[2] Seniors will outnumber children by 2135 and be 22 percent of the population by 2050. There are currently some 50,000 senior resident facilities in the US and that number is rapidly increasing. There's talk of possible future waves of the pandemic or its variants, so who will minister to the seniors then? You see—and here's my next reason for this book—concomitant with the pandemic, there is a shortage of priests. All senior residences will need a book like this. More to the point, so will the parishes.

THE FADING OF THE CLERGY

I slowly began to realize that this wasn't the first time Christians had experienced this problem. In the Church's long history, lay people have always taken up the challenge to keep the Church alive when clergy were not available. Persecution of Christianity's leaders, for example, has been commonplace. Peter and Paul were caught up in Diocletian's persecution. Later, there were the French Revolution and the persecution by Protestant England of the Catholic clergy. The Nazis sent untold numbers of clergy to concentration camps. Add to this the routine plagues that have regularly devastated the globe, such as the fourteenth-century Black Plague that killed some 25 million people, and we realize that periodically the Church has had to exist without sufficient clergy, without whom the essential sacramental and devotional life of the Church could wane and eventually disappear.

Today, in various places around the world where a priest visits perhaps once every two or three months, or even years, the laity has had to take over entirely. In places like the Congo, the laity directs catechesis and bible study, takes over parish leadership, and even celebrates the sacrament of baptism. In some cases, nuns witness marriages. Parish priests in America are stretched to the limits as they celebrate more Masses during

· · · · · · · · · · · · · · · · · ·

2   The Administration for Community Living, *2019 Profile of Older Americans* (Washington, DC: US Department of Health and Human Services, 2020), 11, https://acl.gov/sites/default/files/Aging%20and%20Disability%20in%20America/2019ProfileOlderAmericans508.pdf.

the pandemic because attendance is limited to so few for each Mass. Some pastors today often have to serve three or four parishes. Caring for the faithful in hospitals, nursing homes, and senior residences must be just as spotty.

Nor does the near future look promising, for many seminaries around the world have closed for lack of candidates, projecting an even more likely prospect of life without priests. The average age of US clergy is around 70. Deacons are a great help, but their numbers are declining and they cannot celebrate Mass. That's why there are areas in the United States where laypeople run parishes, catechize, baptize, and preside over Communion Services or Mass without a priest. For example, during the pandemic of 2020, Bishop Thomas Dowd of the Diocese of Sault Sainte Marie, Ontario oversaw the distribution of 12,000 containers of ashes to be sent to the faithful with a brochure containing several prayers that the faithful can recite at home. Laypeople are filling in, holding community together and leading liturgy.

THE DISAPPEARING RELIGIOUS

Formerly, we might not have noticed the clergy shortage as much because we had the ubiquitous nuns that gave us a sense of normalcy. In fact, it is no exaggeration to state that, historically, nuns have made possible a viable and vital Catholicism in our country. They were the real grassroots workers with their invaluable and dynamic presence in our Roman Catholic hospitals and schools.[3] Nuns have been widely engaged in pastoral work, prayer ministries, and various institutions.

In short, the nuns really were the face of the Church and just fifty years ago there were 160,000 of them. Today, they number around 40,000 and most are in their early to late seventies. Sadly, they are dying in large numbers from COVID-19 complications, with no spouse or children to help them, only each other. They

. . . .

3   Additionally, the Roman Catholic school system has and does educate children of color to an extraordinary degree. Supreme Court Justice Sonia Sotomayor, raised in poverty by a single mother, said that Catholic schools have been "a pipeline to opportunity." Los Angeles has the largest Catholic school system in the nation, with more than 70,000 students, 78 percent of them children of color. President Joseph Biden credits the Catholic schools for making him the man he is today.

live in senior residences. In an era when women have entered the workforce in huge numbers and cherish independence, fewer of them are interested in the religious life. So, between the coronavirus deaths, aging, and diminished vocations, religious life is evaporating. Its loss has helped to fade the felt presence of the Church and emphasize the paucity of clergy.

DEATH OF THE CATHOLIC CULTURE

There are also cultural reasons for the present decline of priests and religious. By this, I mean that today there no longer exists a Catholic cultural substratum. There are no overt lingering signals that all will be well. The parochial school system with its uniforms, religious ethos, and celebrations; catechism classes taught by nuns; and a parish church with memorable music, smells, bells, novenas, missions, fish on Friday, and colorful liturgical cycles together produced a cultural Catholicism that found expression in movies about Father O'Malley (*Going My Way*), Father Duffy (World War I hero), Father Francis Chisholm (*Keys of the Kingdom*), and Sister Margaret (*Come to the Stable*). Cherished, memorable rituals and sacred theatre were compelling and comforting. Fr. Vincent Donovan sums it up beautifully:

> The Catholic Church of yesterday had a texture to it, a feel: the smudge of ashes on your forehead on Ash Wednesday, the cool candle against your throat on St. Blaise's day, the waferlike sensation on your tongue in Communion. It had a look: the oddly elegant sight of the silky vestments on the back of the priest as he went about his mysterious rites facing the sanctuary wall in the parish church; the monstrance with its solar radial brilliance surrounding the stark white host of the tabernacle; the indelible impression of the blue-and-white Virgin and the shocking red image of the Sacred Heart. It even had a smell, an odor: the pungent incense, the extinguished candles with their beeswax aroma floating ceilingward

and filling your nostrils, the smell of olive oil and sacramental balm. It had the taste of fish on Fridays and unleavened bread and hot cross buns. It had the sound of unearthly Gregorian chant and *flectamua genua* and the mournful *Dies Irae*. The church had a way of capturing all your senses, keeping your senses enthralled.[4]

All this is gone or has diminished. Cultural Catholicism is dead. Today, Catholic communal identity and solidarity are threatened. The scandals of the 1980s and 90s evaporated any moral standing left for the church. Then, slowly but surely, there followed the closing of parochial schools in large numbers, thus withdrawing an effective way and means of developing cultural Catholicism and leaving the field open to legally secular schooling minus any mention of God. The media, corporate America, and Silicon Valley became hostile to religion. The Church, like all religions, has been ousted from the public square and relegated to "private conscience." Within the Church itself, clericalism has been judged and found wanting. Since the pandemic, so many Catholics watch Mass on TV that they have gotten used to it. Only the very committed are coming back for in-person Mass, leaving some to speculate whether a hybrid Church is the future: a combination of in-person and virtual programs.

So, here we are today, with parents mourning the mass defection of their children and grandchildren from the Church, a deep polarization between liberal and conservative Catholics, the shuttering of schools and churches, the diminishing numbers of nuns and priests, the weight of the clergy sexual scandals, and the added stresses of a pandemic.

PROPHETIC TIMES

All is not lost. Slowly but surely, the people are stepping up because within the bowels of all this negative chaos, hidden

. . . .
4   Vincent J. Donovan, *The Church in the Midst of Creation* (Maryknoll, NY: Orbis, 1989), chapter 1.

in all the turmoil, are tiny seeds of hope. Interested groups are strategizing on how to rebuild the Church. They are cognizant that there is a revolution brewing. Clericalism has come under fire, feminism has refocused the role of women, and baptism has replaced Holy Orders as the premier sacrament. The gifts of the people are coming into focus.

The official Church is moving, however cautiously, into a synodal or prophetic mode, reconfiguring the old pyramid model of the Church into a circular model where more people sit at the decision-making table. For the first time in history, for example, a laywoman is Undersecretary for Relations with States at the Vatican and a layman is the first such person to head a major Vatican department. Laypeople have degrees in theology, scripture, canon law, and community building. There's talk of laypeople having a say in the appointment of bishops. Vatican II's call to "universal holiness" is beginning to catch on. Ideas from Vatican II's Decree on the Apostolate of the Laity are beginning to take hold:

- "Everyone should painstakingly ready himself or herself for the apostolate, especially as an adult." (30)

- "From the reception of these charisms or gifts, including those which are less dramatic, there arise for each believer the right and duty to use them in the Church and the world for the good of humankind and for the upbuilding of the Church." (3)

- "As sharers in the role of Christ the Priest, the Prophet and the King, the laity have an active part to play in the life and activity of the Church." (10)[5]

REFORMATION

We see this most pragmatically in the new approach to priestly formation. Formerly, the model was a severely segre-

....

5   As quoted in United States Catholic Conference, "Called and Gifted: The American Catholic Laity; Reflections of the American Bishops Commemorating the Fifteenth Anniversary of the Issuance of the *Decree on the Apostolate of the Laity*," November 13, 1980, https://www.usccb.org/about/laity-marriage-family-life-and-youth/laity/upload/called_and_gifted.pdf.

gated, all-male monastic one. Seminarians were bleached of any individual local traditions and expressions and hammered into interchangeable parts that could fit in anywhere. It was quite possible that a candidate for bishop, raised and steeped in the moral, intellectual, and sophisticated culture of Boston, would be made bishop of a diocese in Mississippi, whose culture, inside jokes, folklore, and values were foreign to him. That was because the clergy were ordained not only as priests, but as universal practitioners of all things whatsoever. They were the experts, the fathers who knew best.

Today, with clericalism crumbling and with feminism and education commonplace, pastoral leadership has taken on a new definition. With so many laypeople as parish coordinators, spiritual directors, theologians, counselors, and financial experts, and with the increasing role of women in the Church, priestly formation in many places is being carried out in common with laypeople. Seminarians take classes in integrated university settings along with male and female students, or at theological schools attended by men and women who are pursuing vocations in lay ministry. There, they learn to share power. There, they expand their notions of what life, love, family life, virtue, and sin mean to other people.

In short, a Vatican II style of ministry—with the ordained, religious, and lay ministers working together as collaborators— is becoming the new face of the Church. It is significant that the theme of the 2022 Synod of Bishops is, "For a synodal Church: communion, participation, and mission." I would like to suggest that this book is one small aspect of this trend: Laypeople who were formerly deprived or paralyzed by the absence of an ordained priest are now being able to meet the challenges—not under, but alongside the clergy.

For the record, let me add that the Church in practice has always realized this reality and made provisions for it. That is why, from the beginning, the Church has allowed for lay people, with certain restrictions, to fill in during such emergencies. Eventually, this strategy found its way into the Church's Canon Law. Canon 517:2 reads (my emphasis):

> If, because of a lack of priests, the diocesan bishop has decided that participation in the exercise of the pastoral care of a parish is to be entrusted to a deacon, *to another person who is not a priest, or to a community of persons*, he is to appoint some priest who, provided with the powers and faculties of a pastor, is to direct the pastoral care.[6]

What was considered an emergency is becoming standard procedure today. Catholic ministry that used to be limited to the ordained is now a collaborative venture. Understandably, there is a legitimate fear that the mystique and role of the priest may be diminished, but it's my belief that, in time, a better rounded, symbiotic relationship will be established, to the enhancement of the Church and to the priest's emotional, spiritual, and mental health.

We do live in a time of change, a time when the Church is struggling to be relevant again, a time of secularism, pandemic, and diminishing numbers of clergy and religious. But there is a coalition of faithful, intentional Catholics out there, lay and clerical, who, moved by the Spirit, are forging a new way, a new Pentecost. This book is a small part of that effort.

. . . .

6   Book II, 517:2, *Code of Canon Law*, http://www.vatican.va/archive/
cod-iuris-canonici/eng/documents/cic_lib2-cann460-572_en.html.

GUIDELINES FOR USING THIS BOOK

Place. The place for celebrating these liturgies makes a difference. Ideally, they should take place in the parish church, or at least on the parish grounds. The setting, the ambiance, the statues, the architecture—the whole atmosphere helps set a mood, not to mention the convenience of access to microphone and lectern and the presence of the tabernacle. Hopefully, beyond the mask-wearing and social distancing demanded by a bygone pandemic, this allows for a larger group to meet in a religious setting. Even if the group meets in the parish hall, art, banners, or props can reference or enhance the event. The next best thing is to meet in someone's home. If, God forbid, the pandemic is still around, you adjust.

For the elderly living in residences, however, such liturgies, unfortunately, are not and cannot be held in church. Most senior residences do have a chapel, sometimes of a good size, and services ideally can be held there. Should there be too many people to fit into the chapel, or another pandemic demands distancing, then use a hall or auditorium. The downside is that these spaces are not ideal and can be hard to book because many other activities vie for the space. This also means no reverential props, pictures of Jesus or the saints, or whatever religious items could enhance the liturgy—or, if you do have such items, they must be removed before the next event takes place. Still, it can be done. In any case, be sure to reserve the room ahead and set up chairs as strategically as you can.

Singing. Most of the liturgies in this book call for music and singing. However, during pandemic times or other restricting circumstances, do *not* sing, even if participants wear a mask. Singing projects germs farther than normal breathing or talking, and thus is a danger. Therefore, when music or hymns are called for—and you should keep both whenever possible— use either a single cantor or musical background from a piano or recorded music. Music does enhance the liturgy. Note that, in the interest of keeping this book small and manageable, I have not, with a few exceptions, provided suggested hymns.

Flexibility. These liturgies are not written in stone. Feel free to adjust, recreate, and alter them to be more compatible with your needs. You will notice, for instance, that I have rewritten the Passion Gospel on Palm Sunday to make it tighter and given the text more speaking parts. If you find a preferable Stations of the Cross, substitute it. About thirty years ago, Pope John Paul II introduced slightly different stations from the traditional ones, such as omitting Veronica and her veil (which are not scriptural). Also, for example, if the liturgy takes place in a nursing home, you might want to reduce the Stations of the Cross to half: seven instead of fourteen stations. The point is to do whatever will work best for your situation. Participation is essential.

Appendix 1. This appendix contain seasonal homilies. They serve a twofold purpose. First, for the neophyte leader, unsure of what to say, these homilies are available either to be presented verbatim or reworked. In short, they are helpful resources for the leader to tap if necessary. Second, the leader might ask participants who already have this book to read the homilies reflectively beforehand, either the evening before or while waiting for the liturgy to begin, as a spiritual preparation to help them get into a receptive mood.

Connections. Leaders who offer these liturgies in places beyond the parish church should keep in contact with the diocesan Senior Citizens department. The people there will keep you abreast of what's happening universally from a Catholic viewpoint. Keep in contact also with the local parish. This way, you can find out if a priest or deacon is available so you know which option to choose. Likewise, where Communion services without a priest are used, the local parish will be the source of consecrated hosts. Also, contact helpful groups like the Altar-Rosary Society, or Men's Guild, or Knights of Columbus so they may help you with your needs. For example, they might donate small Advent wreaths, underwrite bulk purchases of this book so everyone can have a copy, or provide other resources that are beyond your capacity.

A Note about Apprehension. Perhaps some seniors raised in a clergy-dominated Church may feel uneasy with leading or praying with a congregation of people without a priest present, feeling somehow that it's not legitimate. They remember that Pope Pius XI was quick to define Catholic Action as "the participation of the laity in the apostolate of the bishops" to be sure the laity knew where it stood. The bishops concurred. To their credit, at Vatican II, the bishops repented of such arrogance and bad theology and, going back to Christian foundations, reasserted baptism as the primary sacrament which conferred the Holy Spirit and made all people "Church," each with his or her own gifts by virtue of that baptism. In fact, the US Bishops, in one of their more inspired moments, issued a Decree on the Apostolate of the Laity in November 1980. Reflecting on Vatican II, they wrote:

> One of the chief characteristics of lay men and women today is their growing sense of being adult members of the Church . . . called to exercise the same sure interdependence and practical self-direction that characterize them in other areas of life. . . . Baptism and confirmation empower all believers to share in some form of ministry. . . . Since the Second Vatican Council, new opportunities have developed for lay men and women to serve in the Church.[1]

So, put aside any reservations and, in these unsettled times, keep alive the customs, devotions, and liturgies that have always nourished the faithful. As for those places in this book where a reflection or homily is indicated, just be yourself. Speak from the heart or share some wisdom from spiritual reading you have come across. Again, do note that, for some high-profile instances, I have offered homilies in Appendix 1 that will be helpful.

· · · · · · · · · · · · · · · · ·

1   USCC, "Called and Gifted."

THE WIDER CONTEXT

I close these introductory chapters with two spiritual reminders, thoughts to keep subconsciously close to your heart as a Catholic and as a member of the Communion of Saints. The first is this: As you freely meet to pray and celebrate in reasonable safety and comfort, don't forget your fellow Christians around the world who meet and celebrate in utter fear. The following summary by John L. Allen, Jr. makes the case and should occasionally be re-read:

> When two suicide bombers detonated their devices outside a Palm Sunday Mass [on March 28, 2021 at the Sacred Heart of Jesus Cathedral in Indonesia], they were the only ones who died, in part because a security guard had prevented them from entering the church's compound.
>
> At least twenty people were wounded, but because no one other than the attackers actually lost their lives, the incident probably won't cause much of a ripple in global interest.
>
> It doesn't really compare to the Easter Sunday bombings in Sri Lanka two years [prior], for instance, which targeted Christian churches and high-end hotels, leaving 269 people dead and hundreds more injured. . . .
>
> Every year on major Christian feast days, somewhere in the world, Christians will be killed for no reason other than that they chose to attend religious services. Because Christmas and Holy Week are the holiest periods on the Christian calendar, churches tend to be especially full, presenting ripe targets for anti-Christian hatred. . . .
>
> In 2012, a car bomb exploded near a church in Kaduna, Nigeria, while Easter was being celebrated, killing 41 people in an attack suspected of being the work of the Islamist extremist group

Boko Haram. In 2016, 75 people died and more than 300 were injured when bombs exploded in a park in Lahore, Pakistan, as Christians were celebrating after Easter services. The following year, Coptic Christians in Egypt were forced to scale back Easter celebrations after bombings at two churches on Palm Sunday the week before, which opens the Easter observances, killed more than 40 people.

A similar pattern applies to Christmas. In 2011, for example, Boko Haram claimed responsibility for bombings across Nigeria on the holiday, including an attack on St. Theresa Catholic Church in Madalla, on the outskirts of Nigeria's capital city, Abuja, that left 37 people dead and 57 injured. . . .

Although Christians are simply one among a staggering set of vulnerable minority groups around the world exposed to hatred and persecution, there remains a sort of wall of silence around their suffering. In part, that's because the people who set the tone in global politics and the media generally live in the affluent West, where Christians generally don't encounter much physical persecution. . . .

That neglect reflects a terribly superannuated grasp of the Christian map. More than two-thirds of the 2.3 billion Christians today live outside the West, most in developing societies and often not only religious but also ethnic and linguistic minorities. Most are poor, and the majority are women.

Because of that, and because Christians are the largest religious group on the planet, the raw numbers in terms of anti-Christian persecution are staggering. Estimates of how many Christians are killed yearly around the world because of their faith vary widely, from thousands to tens of thousands, but it's a statistical certainty that at any hour of the day, a Christian somewhere is being martyred.[2]

Again, as we gather in reasonable safety and comfort for our liturgies, let us keep in our hearts our brothers and sisters who gather in fear and anxiety.

My second reminder is a homiletic version of the same thought.

ALL SAINTS

This feast is clearly a gorgeous paean to God's mercy, to God's all-inclusiveness. The rousing song *When the Saints Go Marching In* rightly provokes inspiring and truly awesome feelings. Recall the exotic readings proclaimed at this feast, which conjure up a great heavenly panoramic scene of vast multitudes of 144,000 saints, multiplied endlessly. That endless crowd invokes many marvelous and compelling images—none more powerful, I suggest, than that of a heavenly chorus. Yes, close your eyes for a moment and picture yourself standing in that chorus of endless multiples of 144,000 people, singing a song of faith; singing aloud, if you will, the Creed. Then I ask you to be aware of two things that will be operating as each of us belts out our song.

The first is this: No one believes it all. That's right: No one believes it all. Each of us in the chorus is gifted with only a partial understanding of the mystery of God among us. Therefore, in our large chorus, one sings a certain part with great intensity and assurance, while another sings with little intention and conviction. That's OK. No one believes it all, but, together, we proclaim more than we can proclaim alone. Together, we sing more than we can sing alone.

And so the saints, you see, the saints are a chorus, a communion that sings what we cannot and believes those parts we struggle to accept. They chant the song of faith with us when we can join them and they hum the song of faith when we can-

. . . .

2   John L. Allen, Jr., "A Reminder that Holy Week Is Prime Time for Anti-Christian Violence," *Crux*, March 29, 2021, https://cruxnow.com/news-analysis/2021/03/a-reminder-that-holy-week-is-prime-time-for-anti-christian-violence/.

not. Together, we, the saints of yesterday and today, sing more than we can sing alone, for no one believes it all—but all believe.

The second operating element is this: If no one believes it all, so also no one believes all the time. Our journey of faith is seldom smooth and uninterrupted. At times, it fluctuates between belief and unbelief. Perhaps today we're caught by the words and melody because we happen to be in a good place, emotionally and spiritually. But, another time, in another mental or emotional place, we may feel doubtful and alienated and can hardly get the words out of our mouths.

A few years ago, a friend of mine lost her son in an automobile accident. She says that she can no longer believe in God, in a God who would let her son lose his life, especially since she and her family are faithful Catholics and good churchgoers. How could God do this to her?

There are three responses to this woman. The first is to say, "Well, if you can no longer believe, you are no longer a Catholic. You no longer belong." That's a harsh view. That denies the seriousness of her loss. A second response is to say to her, "You haven't really lost your faith. You're just temporarily depressed. Everything will be fine." But everything will *not* be fine. This response denies her pain. But the third response is to honor her losses: the loss of her son, the loss of—or at least the shock to—her faith. The fact of the matter is that tragedy has indeed broken her trust in a loving, provident God.

Meanwhile? Meanwhile, the community believes *for* her. The saintly chorus picks up her faltering verses. The collective faith of the saints sustains her though her period of unbelief. As she slowly encounters these saints of yesterday and today, she will begin to see *their* scars and sense *their* resilience. Over time, they will help her believe once more, in the face of tragic absurdity, in a new and different way. They will help her sing with a different modulation. They will sing more loudly the phrases that she can only sing softly, if at all.

So, you see, no one—you or I—believes it all. And no one here believes all the time. No one accepts every verse, and no one can sing every note all the time. But the chorus does. The chorus, or the community of saints, sings when you and I are unwilling or unable to do so. Peter sang for Doubting Thomas until he could believe again. Thomas sang for Denying Peter until he could embrace again. Monica sang for her son, Augustine, when he was in his period of sinfulness and unbelief, until he could repent and sing again. When Francis was sad, Clare sang for him until he was glad again. We are a whole community. We are a chorus of saints. We support each other and we become more than the sum total of our individual selves.

You exhibit the gifts I don't have, and I exhibit those you don't have. You cry the tears I cannot cry and I laugh the laughter you cannot laugh. You believe when I struggle with doubts. I believe when you struggle with doubts. You smile while I am in tragedy. I grieve while you are in joy. Our individual pieces are partial. Our faith, our hope, and our love are quite incomplete. But the feast of the saints, of *all* the saints—past, present, and future, those in heaven, earth, and purgatory—tells us something. This feast gives us support. It reminds us of our faith family, that we belong to a vast community of time and space. It becomes a revelation and a comfort. It tells us a mighty, comforting truth: Together, we sing more than we can sing alone.[3]

The themes of spiritual camaraderie, connection, and compassion should never be far from our hearts whenever we use this book. Meanwhile, do remember:

Conversations will not be cancelled.
Relationships will not be cancelled.
Love will not be cancelled.
Songs will not be cancelled.
Reading will not be cancelled.
Self-care will not be cancelled.
Hope will not be cancelled.[4]

—Jamie Tworkowski

. . . .

3   A version of this homily was previously published in William J. Bausch, *An Anthology of Saints: Official, Unofficial, and Would-be Saints* (New London, CT: Twenty-Third Publications, 2012), 8–10.

4   Jamie Tworkowski, "Hope Will Not Be Cancelled," *TWLOHA*, March 15, 2020, https://twloha.com/blog/hope-will-not-be-cancelled/.

The LITURGIES

The BLESSING OF THE ADVENT WREATH

Advent, a winter season for most of us, is a time marker, a slow approach to the Birth of Christ. With the Advent wreath's four candles (three purple and one pink), one more lit each week, the Light becomes brighter, the yearning more intense, its evergreens generating hope. In any senior residence you can create your own ritual, knowing that you are joining with Christians around the world in this sacred season.

Some creative people can gather their own evergreens and make their own personal wreaths. For seniors living in community, of course, there can be no real candles since fire is always a danger, but they can use homemade paper candles or battery-sourced flames. For a communal service, one large, prominent wreath, either homemade or bought, is all that is needed. To find out where to purchase a large wreath, search online or contact your local parish. They may even donate a wreath through one of their organizations.

This blessing of the wreath is a one-time celebration at the beginning of Advent.

OPENING HYMN *(sung or recited)*

O come, O come Emmanuel,
and ransom captive Israel,
that mourns in lonely exile here,
until the Son of God appear.
  Rejoice! rejoice! Emmanuel
  shall come to you, O Israel!

O come, thou Wisdom, from on high,
and order all things far and nigh;
to us the path of knowledge show,
and cause us in her ways to go.
  Rejoice! Rejoice! Emmanuel
  shall come to you, O Israel!

Leader: Before we begin, allow me to share some background as we prepare to celebrate this brief blessing of the Advent wreath and our anticipation of Christmas itself. We begin by citing the obvious truth: no one knows exactly when Jesus Christ was born, so how did we wind up with December 25th?

The answer is as follows. The Christian church, as you know, has its own calendar. In the church's calendar, the new year begins with the first Sunday of Advent, the season which leads us to Christmas. But Christmas and Advent are wonderfully repurposed pagan feasts. So, going to back to pagan times, when these celebrations started, will give us spiritual insight into this season.

Here's the way it worked. The pagans saw the world as a great cosmic struggle between the powers of darkness and the powers of light. And they noticed, as they watched the battle in the skies, that darkness seemed to be getting the better of the light at certain times. In fact, it seemed to them that they were watching two great cosmic wrestlers. Every once in a while, they would see that the wrestler called "darkness" would pin down the wrestler called "light" and be ready to do it in. They surmised this because they could plainly see that the days at this time of the year were getting shorter. If days were getting shorter, that meant that the light, or the sun, was fading. It meant that, as darkness pinned the sun onto its back—and was ready to dispatch it, so to speak—the sun, the light, was getting weaker. Yes, it was obvious that those fearful, dark days were getting stronger and longer. They were afraid that someday darkness would kill the sun and the light altogether. They shuddered in fear—that is, until around December 21st.

Around December 21st, they noticed something. They noticed that the tables had begun to turn, and that the sun was regaining its strength. It appeared that the hero, who was pinned down on the ground with an adversary over him, got a second wind and was beginning to push off darkness. To them, this meant that darkness was getting weaker and the sun was getting stronger. When this happened, the pagans celebrated the resurrection, or the new birth, of the sun. It was, for them, a sun feast, marking the transition time from the prominence of darkness to the return of light.

Enter the Christians. When they came along, they took over this fascinating pagan notion. They said, "We don't know the exact date Christ was born, but if we're going to have to pick out one, this time of the year is perfect. After all, we know that the pagans are really talking about darkness and light, and we know that the only real darknesses of this world are the darkness of sin and the darkness of death. And the only light in this world is Jesus. So, we'll keep the concept and fix his birthday right after December 21st, when the light is starting to return."

So, the Christians settled on December 25th. In English, they also took the word "sun," removed the middle letter, "u," and changed it to "o." So, the sun they were talking about that overcame the darkness was Jesus, the Son of God. They made this time of year a celebration, when Christians would get ready for the tables to be turned and light to strengthen again.

So, in the Christian scheme, in the great struggle between good and evil, light and darkness, this was the time when the darkness of sin and death would now be overcome by the light of the world: Jesus, the S-o-n of God. And they delighted in playing on the light-darkness themes, such as quoting Isaiah 9:2, which states that "from the darkness, a great light has risen among us." And how could they not often quote the wonderful and powerful words of Saint Paul, who wrote,

> It is now the hour for you to wake from sleep, for our salvation is closer than when we first accepted the faith. The night is far spent, the day draws near. Let us cast off deeds of darkness and put on the armor of light. Let us live honorably as in daylight, not in carousing and drunkenness, not in sexual excess and lust, not in quarrelling and jealousy. Rather, put on the Lord Jesus Christ and make no room for selfish desires of the heart. (Romans 13:11–14)

So, the Christians called this time Christmas, and they made Advent the weeks approaching the end of darkness and looking forward to the coming light. That's what it has meant to us Christians ever since. Advent marks that time when darkness is strongest, but begins to grow weaker as the sun becomes stronger. It is a time for us to repent and let in the light.[1]

With this history in mind, let us begin our blessing with a reading from the book of Isaiah (61:1–2):

The spirit of the Lord is upon me, because he has anointed me to preach good news to the poor. He has sent me to bind up the brokenhearted, to proclaim freedom for the captives and release from darkness for the prisoners, to proclaim the year of the Lord's favor and the day of vengeance of our God; to comfort all who mourn and provide for those who grieve.

The word of the Lord:

Chorus: Thanks be to God.

THE LITANY OF ADVENT

Leader:	**Chorus:**
Lord Jesus, you are the light of the world.	*Come, Lord Jesus.*
Lord Jesus, you are light in our darkness.	*Come, Lord Jesus.*
Son of God, save us from our selfishness.	*Come, Lord Jesus.*
Loving Savior, bring hope to the hopeless.	*Come, Lord Jesus.*
Give your peace and justice to all nations.	*Come, Lord Jesus.*
Joy of all who love you,	*Come, Lord Jesus.*
Unity to all who believe in you,	*Come, Lord Jesus.*
Christ, whose coming we await,	*Come, Lord Jesus.*
Comfort of the Father,	*Come, Lord Jesus.*
Healing of the Spirit,	*Come, Lord Jesus.*
Grandson to Anne and Joachim,	*Come, Lord Jesus.*
Strength of youth and weakness of the old,	*Come, Lord Jesus.*
Holy Presence, stay with us always.	*Come, Lord Jesus.*

1   A version of this reflection was previously published in William J. Bausch, *Telling Stories, Compelling Stories* (Mystic, CT: Twenty-Third Publications, 1991), 132–137.

Leader: Let us pray:

O God, we yearn for your holy presence. Our hearts are full of expectation of your comfort, now and at the hour of our death. You are the One who makes all things new again. Come, Lord Jesus.

Chorus: Amen.

Leader: Now listen to the Canticle of Zechariah from the Gospel of Luke (1:67–79):

At that time Zechariah proclaimed: Blessed be the Lord God of Israel, for he has looked with favor on his people and redeemed them. He has raised up a mighty Savior for us in the house of David, his servant, as he foretold through the prophets that we would be saved from our enemies and from the hand of all who hate us. Thus the Lord God has shown the mercy he promised to our ancestors. He has not forgotten his holy covenant or the oath that he swore to Abraham, that we would serve him without fear and in righteousness before him, all our days. Yes, by the tender mercy of our God, the dawn from on high will soon break upon us to give the light to those who sit in darkness and in the shadow of death.

The Gospel of the Lord.

Chorus: Praise to you, Lord Jesus Christ.

Here a reflection may be shared. (See Appendix 1 for homily resource.)

After the reflection, the Leader moves toward the Advent wreath and prays:

Leader: Lord our God,
we praise you for your Son, Jesus Christ:
He is Emmanuel, the hope of the peoples,
he is the wisdom that teaches and guides us,
he is the Savior of every nation.
Lord God, let your blessing come upon us
as we light the candles of this wreath.
May the wreath and its light
be a sign of Christ's promise to bring us salvation.
May he come quickly and not delay.
We ask this through Christ our Lord.

Chorus: Amen.

Leader: O God, by whose Word all things are sanctified, pour forth your blessing upon this wreath and grant that we who use it may prepare our hearts for the coming of Christ and may receive from you abundant graces. We ask this through Christ our Lord.

Chorus: Amen.

Leader: The blessing is ended. Go in peace.

Chorus: Thanks be to God.

Here you may exit in silence or while repeating the opening hymn.

For private use in your own house or apartment, the following Advent wreath prayers can be used.[2] Each week a new candle is lit (literally or figuratively), adding to the preceding ones, and a new prayer is added.

FIRST WEEK

O Lord, stir up your might, we beg you, and come, that by your protection we may deserve to be rescued from the

2   These prayers are the traditional collects for each Sunday in Advent.

threatening dangers of our sins and saved by your deliverance. Through Christ our Lord. Amen.

The candle is allowed to burn during evening meals for the first week.

SECOND WEEK

O Lord, stir up our hearts, that we may prepare for your only begotten Son, that through His coming we may be made worthy to serve you with pure minds. Through Christ our Lord. Amen.

The two candles are allowed to burn during the evening meals of the second week.

THIRD WEEK

O Lord, we beg you, incline your ear to our prayers and enlighten the darkness of our minds by the grace of your visitation. Through Christ our Lord. Amen.

The three candles are allowed to burn during the evening meals of the third week.

FOURTH WEEK

O Lord, stir up your power, we pray you, and come; and with great might help us, that with the help of your Grace, your merciful forgiveness may hasten what our sins impede. Through Christ our Lord. Amen.

The four candles are allowed to burn during the evening meals of the fourth week.

CHRISTMAS DAY

There is something unsettling about not being able to go to church on Christmas and no amount of alternate liturgy can spiritually or emotionally substitute for it. Taking part in a liturgy outside the church building can seem a contradiction, a letdown. It's like eating Thanksgiving dinner by yourself. Still, we make do with what we have, where we are. There will no doubt be Christmas decorations where we live, and we ourselves can still have song, prayer, scripture, and the crèche as best we can. We have each other. We can sing songs that express our faith. The following Christmas liturgy presumes the presence of a priest, but concludes with adaptations in case a priest cannot be present.

Leader: Welcome to this joyous occasion where we, like the lowly shepherds, have gathered at our own manger to show awe and gratitude and to give praise. So, let us begin this wonderful occasion by singing one verse of "O Little Town of Bethlehem":

Chorus: O little town of Bethlehem,
how still we see thee lie;
above thy deep and dreamless sleep
the silent stars go by.
Yet in thy dark streets shineth
the everlasting Light;
the hopes and fears of all the years
are met in thee tonight.

Celebrant: Let us begin our worship together in the name of the Father and of the Son and of the Holy Spirit.

Chorus: Amen.

Celebrant: The grace of our Lord Jesus Christ and the love of God and the communion of the Holy Spirit be with you all.

Chorus: And also with you.

Celebrant: My brothers and sisters, to prepare ourselves to take part in this sacred liturgy, let us first call to mind our sins:

Chorus: I confess to Almighty God,
　　　　　and to you, my brothers and sisters,
　　　　　that I have greatly sinned,
　　　　　in my thoughts and in my words,
　　　　　in what I have done and in what I have failed
　　　　　　　to do,
　　　　　through my fault, through my fault, through
　　　　　　　my most grievous fault.
　　　　　Therefore I ask Blessed Mary ever-virgin,
　　　　　all the angels and saints,
　　　　　and you my brothers and sisters
　　　　　to pray for me to the Lord our God.

Celebrant: May Almighty God have mercy on us, forgive us our sins, and bring us to life everlasting. Amen.

Chorus: Glory to God in the highest
　　　　　and peace to his people on earth.
　　　　　Lord God, heavenly King,
　　　　　Almighty God and Father.
　　　　　We worship you, we give you thanks,
　　　　　we praise you for your glory.
　　　　　Lord Jesus Christ, only Son of the Father,
　　　　　Lord God, Lamb of God,
　　　　　you take away the sin of the world,
　　　　　have mercy on us.
　　　　　You are seated at the right hand of the Father,

receive our prayer.
For you alone are the Holy One,
you alone are the Lord,
you alone are the Most High,
Jesus Christ, with the Holy Spirit,
in the glory of God the Father. Amen.

Celebrant: Let us pray [*short pause here*]: With our brothers and sisters gathered this day in cathedrals, churches, and hidden places throughout the world, we rejoice, for a child is born for us and a Son is given to us. God's eternal word has leapt down from heaven in the silent watches of the night and now we are forever filled with the wonder of the nearness of God. We pray that God will open our hearts to receive his life and increase our vision that our hope may overflow the limits of our bodies and we be filled with his glory and his peace.

Chorus: Amen.

Leader: A reading from the prophet Isaiah (9:2, 6–7):
The people who walked in darkness have seen
a great light;
upon those who dwelt in the land of gloom, a
light has shone.
For a child is born to us, a Son is given us;
upon his shoulder, dominion rests.
They name him Wonder-Counselor, God-
Hero, Father-Forever,
and Prince of Peace.
His dominion is vast and forever peaceful.
From David's throne and over his kingdom,
which he confirms and
sustains by judgment and justice, he rules
both now and forever.
The word of the Lord.

Chorus: Thanks be to God.

RESPONSORIAL PSALM *(Psalm 96:1–3, 11–13)*

Leader: Today is born our Savior, Christ the Lord.

Chorus: Today is born our Savior, Christ the Lord.

Leader: Sing to the Lord a new song,
      sing to the Lord, all you lands.
      Sing to the Lord, bless his name.

Chorus: Today is born our Savior, Christ the Lord.

Leader: Announce his salvation, day after day.
      Tell his glory among the nations,
      among all peoples, his wondrous deeds.

Chorus: Today is born our Savior, Christ the Lord.

Leader: Let the heavens be glad and the earth rejoice,
      let the sea and the waters resound;
      let the plains be joyful and all that is in them;
      then shall all the trees in the forest exult.

Chorus: Today is born our Savior, Christ the Lord.

Leader: They shall exult before the Lord for he comes,
      for he comes to rule the earth.
      He shall rule the earth with justice
      and the people with his constancy.

Chorus: Today is born our Savior, Christ the Lord.

Leader: A reading from Saint Paul to Titus (2:11–14):

The grace of God has appeared, offering salvation to all. It trains us to reject godless ways and worldly desires and live temperately, justly, and devoutly in this age as we await our blessed hope, the appearing of the glory of the great God and of our Savior Christ Jesus. It was he who sacrificed himself for us, to redeem us from all unrighteousness and to cleanse for himself a people of his own, eager to do what is right.

The word of the Lord.

Chorus: Thanks be to God.

Celebrant: The Lord be with you.

Chorus: And with your spirit.

Celebrant: The Holy Gospel according to Luke (2:1–14).

Chorus: Glory to you, O God.

Celebrant: In those days, Caesar Augustus published a decree ordering a census of the whole world. The first census took place while Quirinius was governor of Syria. Everyone went to resister, each to his own town. And so Joseph went from the town of Nazareth in Galilee to Judea, to David's town of Bethlehem, because he was of the house and lineage of David, to resister with Mary, his espoused wife, who was with child. When they were there, the days of her confinement were completed. She gave birth to her first-born and wrapped him in swaddling clothes and laid him in a manger because there was no room for them in the place where travelers lodged.

Now, there were shepherds in the locality, living in the fields and keeping night watch by turns over their flock. The angel of the Lord appeared to them as the glory of the Lord shone around them and they were very much afraid. The angel said to them, "You have nothing to fear! I come to proclaim good news to you—tidings of great joy to be shared by the whole people. This day, in David's city, a savior has been born to you. In a manger, you will find an infant wrapped in swaddling clothes." Suddenly, there was with the angel a multitude of the heavenly host, praising God and saying, "Glory to God in high heaven and peace on earth to those on whom his favor rests."

The gospel of the Lord.

Chorus: Praise to you, Lord Jesus Christ.

THE HOMILY *(You may use the one in Appendix 1.)*

THE APOSTLES' CREED

(Here and in later liturgies, we will use the Apostles' Creed to avoid dancing around the still-unedited Nicene Creed with its exclusive language; for example, "For us men and for our salvation he came down from heaven and by the Holy Spirit was incarnate of the Virgin Mary, and became man.")

Chorus: I believe in God
    the Father Almighty,
    Creator of heaven and earth,
    and in Jesus Christ, his only Son, our Lord,
    who was conceived by the Holy Spirit,
    born of the Virgin Mary,
    suffered under Pontius Pilate,
    was crucified, died, and was buried.
    He descended into hell.
    On the third day he rose again from the dead;
    he ascended into heaven
    and is seated at the right hand of God the
        Father Almighty.
    From there he will come to judge the living
        and the dead.
    I believe in the Holy Spirit,
    the Holy Catholic Church,
    the communion of saints,
    the forgiveness of sins,
    the resurrection of the body,
    and life everlasting. Amen.

PRAYERS OF THE FAITHFUL
(Feel free to create your own)

Leader: In our prayers of the faithful, let us remember all those in need.

For Christians gathered everywhere this day, in public or in secret, may the light of Christ give hope to all, let us pray to the Lord.

Chorus: Lord, hear our prayer.

Leader: For the lonely, the ill, the confined, the suffering, the abandoned: may the One who took on our human condition give them compassion and hope, let us pray to the Lord.

Chorus: Lord, hear our prayer.

Leader: That a world that sits in darkness may be renewed by the Light that is Christ, let us pray to the Lord.

Chorus: Lord, hear our prayer.

Leader: That our leaders in government and in church may strive for the justice and truth that the Prince of Peace came to give, let us pray to the Lord.

Chorus: Lord, hear our prayer.

Leader: That the gifts of family, friends, caregivers, and advocates for peace, wholeness, and reconciliation remind us of your saving presence, let us pray to the Lord.

Chorus: Lord, hear our prayer.

Leader: That a sustaining faith, a fragile hope, and a faltering but felt love that overcomes all things may be our deepest Christmas gifts, let us pray to the Lord.

Chorus: Lord, hear our prayer.

Leader: For the sick and the needy of our community and for all those who have died in Christ, especially those near and dear to us, let us pray to the Lord.

Chorus: Lord, hear our prayer.

Celebrant: Here you may add your own intentions. *(pause)*
Almighty God, listen to the prayers of your gathered Church and grant all those things for which we cry out from the depth of our being, through Christ our Lord.

Chorus: Amen.

If a priest is present, Mass continues as normal from this point.

If there is no priest present, proceed directly to the Our Father, followed by the prayers below. You may wish to conclude with an exit hymn. This will be the routine for a Communion Service for all subsequent liturgies in this book.

Leader: Deliver us, Lord, we pray, from every evil,
graciously grant peace in our days, so that,
by the help of your mercy, we may always be
free from sin
and safe from all distress as we await the
blessed hope
and the coming of our Savior, Jesus Christ.

Chorus: For the kingdom, the power, and the glory are yours, now and for ever.

Leader: Lord Jesus Christ, who said to your Apostles:
Peace I leave you, my peace I give you,
look not on our sins, but on the faith of
your Church,
and graciously grant her peace and unity
in accordance with your will,
who live and reign for ever and ever.

Chorus: Amen.

Leader: The peace of the Lord be with you always.

Chorus: And with your spirit.

Leader: Let us offer each other the sign of peace. (*in whatever manner that might safely be.*)

Leader and Chorus:
Lamb of God, you take away the sins of the world,
have mercy on us.
Lamb of God, you take away the sins of the world,
have mercy on us.
Lamb of God, you take away the sins of the world,
grant us peace.

INVITATION TO COMMUNION

Leader: Behold the Lamb of God,
behold him who takes away the sins of
the world.
Blessed are those called to the supper of
the Lamb.

Chorus: Lord, I am not worthy that you should enter
under my roof,
but only say the word and my soul shall
be healed.

Distribution of Communion follows.

CONCLUDING RITES

Leader: The Lord be with you.

Chorus: And with your spirit.

Leader: May almighty God bless us, the Father, and the Son, +
and the Holy Spirit.

Chorus: Amen.

Leader: The Mass is ended. Go in peace.

Chorus: Thanks be to God.

Some may wish to end with the blessing of the crèche. This
could also be done at the beginning of the liturgy.

Leader: God of every nation and people, from the very beginning of creation you have made manifest your love. When our
need for a Savior was great, you sent your Son to be born of
the Virgin Mary. To our lives he brings joy and peace, justice,
mercy, and love.

Lord, bless all who look upon this manger; may it remind us of the humble birth of Jesus and raise up our thoughts to him, who is God-with-us and Savior of all, and who lives and reigns for ever and ever.

Chorus: Amen.

CLOSING HYMN

Silent night, holy night!
All is calm, all is bright.
Round yon virgin mother and child,
holy Infant so tender and mild,
sleep in heavenly peace.
Sleep in heavenly peace.

Silent night, holy night.
Shepherds quake at the sight;
glories stream from heaven afar,
heav'nly hosts sing "Alleluia!"
Christ the Savior is born!
Christ the Savior is born!

FEAST OF THE EPIPHANY

Epiphany is usually celebrated twelve days after Christmas, although some places move it to the nearest Sunday. It's a wonderfully exotic feast: mysterious Wise Men from the East, a traveling star, a wicked king, stunning presents—it's no wonder that storytelling has had a field day with the Magi, in time transmuted into three specific kings. This holy day doesn't get much play in America—meaning there are no special sales that day! But it is a huge festival for most Latino peoples, who know it as the Festival of the Three Kings (*Fiesta de los tres Reyes Magos*), where the Wise Men, dressed in costume, give out presents and special treats of cakes and cookies.

However celebrated, it carries deeper meanings, with the Magi seen as the precursors of gentiles coming into the Church, a paradigm of a Pilgrim People often persecuted, and a light to others. With a nod to the Latino traditions, participants might want to bring small, nicely wrapped presents to the celebration—perhaps a dollar bill, some coins, a trinket or small keepsake—and lay them on a table to be picked up by others on the way out. If feasible, perhaps a large classic painting of the Adoration of the Magi might be projected on a screen for the occasion. For liturgies taking place within churches, a whiff of incense might be appropriate.

OPENING HYMN *(sung or played)*

We three kings of Orient are
bearing gifts, we traverse afar,
field and fountain,
moor and mountain,
following yonder star.

O star of wonder, star of night,
star with royal beauty bright;
westward leading,
still proceeding,
guide us to thy perfect light!

Born a King on Bethlehem's plain;   *O star of wonder, star of night,*
gold I bring to crown him again.   *star with royal beauty bright;*
King forever,   *westward leading,*
ceasing never,   *still proceeding,*
over us all to reign.   *guide us to thy perfect light!*

Celebrant: Let us begin our worship together in the name of the Father and of the Son and of the Holy Spirit.

Chorus: Amen.

Celebrant: The grace of our Lord Jesus Christ and the love of God and the communion of the Holy Spirit be with you all.

Chorus: And also with you.

Celebrant: My brothers and sisters, to prepare ourselves to take part in this sacred liturgy, let us first call to mind our sins: *(pause)*

Chorus: I confess to Almighty God,
and to you, my brothers and sisters,
that I have greatly sinned,
in my thoughts and in my words,
in what I have done and in what I have failed
   to do,
through my fault, through my fault, through
   my most grievous fault.
Therefore I ask Blessed Mary ever-virgin,
all the angels and saints,
and you my brothers and sisters
to pray for me to the Lord our God.

Celebrant: May Almighty God have mercy on us, forgive us our sins, and bring us to life everlasting. Amen.

Chorus: Glory to God in the highest
and peace to his people on earth.
Lord God, heavenly King,
Almighty God and Father.
We worship you, we give you thanks,
we praise you for your glory.

Lord Jesus Christ, only Son of the Father,
Lord God, Lamb of God,
you take away the sin of the world,
Have mercy on us.
You are seated at the right hand of the Father,
receive our prayer.
For you alone are the Holy One,
you alone are the Lord,
you alone are the Most High,
Jesus Christ, with the Holy Spirit,
in the glory of God the Father, Amen.

Leader: Let us pray. *(silence)*

Gracious God, the star that led the Magi to the stable announced to the world that its Savior was born. Today we find ourselves living in a world that is still covered by division and darkness, death and despair. We still need to make that journey to the stable door and show others the way. May our lives be like the stars, reflecting your light and guiding those who are seeking you, whether they know it or not. Sustain us in our journey and help us to serve where you have placed us. We ask this through Christ our Lord.

Chorus: Amen.

Leader: A reading from the book of the prophet Isaiah (60:1–6):

Rise up in splendor, O Jerusalem, for your light has come and the glory of the Lord shines upon you. Darkness covers the earth and thick clouds your people, but upon you the Lord shines and over you appears his glory. Nations shall walk by your light and kings by your shining radiance. So, raise your eyes and look around you: Your sons are coming from afar and your infant daughters are in the arms of their nurses. You will be joyous at what you see and your hearts will throb. The riches of the sea shall be emptied out before you and the wealth of nations brought to you. Yes, caravans of camels shall fill you and dromedaries come from Midian and Ephah. All from the land of Sheba shall come, bearing gold and frankincense and proclaiming the praises of the Lord.

This is the word of the Lord.

Chorus: Thanks be to God.

RESPONSORIAL PSALM
(Psalm 72:1–2, 7–8, 10–13)

Leader: Lord, every nation on earth will adore you.

Chorus: Lord, every nation on earth will adore you.

Leader: O God, with your judgment endow the king,
    and with your justice the king's son.
    He shall govern your people with justice
    and your afflicted ones with judgment.

Chorus: Lord, every nation on earth will adore you.

Leader: Justice shall flower in his days
    and profound peace till the moon shine
        no more.
    May he rule from sea to sea,
    and from the river to the ends of the earth.

Chorus: Lord, every nation on earth will adore you.

Leader: The kings of Tarshish and the Isles shall offer
        you gifts;
    the kings of Arabia and Seba shall bring tribute.
    All kings shall pay him homage,
    all nations shall serve him.

Chorus: Lord, every nation on earth will adore you.

Leader: For he shall rescue the poor when they cry out
    and the afflicted when they have no one to
        help them.
    He shall have pity for the lowly and poor,
    the lives of the poor he shall save.

Chorus: Lord, every nation on earth will adore you.

Leader: A reading from the letter of Paul to the Ephesians (3:2–3a, 5–6):

My friends: I am sure that by this time you have heard of the ministry which God in his goodness gave me on your behalf. God's secret plan, as I have already briefly described to you, was revealed to me, a plan unknown to others in former times but, in these times, revealed by the Spirit to the holy apostles and prophets. And that plan is no less than this: In Christ Jesus, the Gentiles are now co-heirs with the Jews! Yes, they too are members of the same body and sharers of the same promise through the preaching of the gospel.

The word of the Lord.

Chorus: Thanks be to God.

Leader: A reading from the Holy Gospel according to Matthew (2:1–12):

After Jesus' birth in Bethlehem during Herod's reign, Magi from the East arrived one day in Jerusalem. They were inquiring where to find the newborn king of the Jews, saying that they had observed his star at its rising. They came, they said, to pay him homage. This news alarmed Herod and all of Jerusalem with him, so Herod summoned all of the chief priests and the scribes, inquiring of them where the Messiah was to be born. They quickly informed him, "Why, in Bethlehem of Judea. Here are the words of the prophet: 'And you, Bethlehem, land of Judah, are by no means the least among the princes of Judah, since from you shall come a ruler who is to shepherd my people Israel.'"

Herod discreetly called the Magi aside, asking exactly the time of the star's appearance. Then he sent them on to Bethlehem after telling them, "Go and get detailed information about this child. When you have discovered something, come back and report your findings to me so that I too may go and offer him homage."

After their audience with Herod, the Magi set out once more. They were overjoyed to see that the star which they had observed at its rising went ahead of them until it came to a standstill over the place where the child was. Upon entering, they found the child with Mary, his mother. Immediately, they prostrated themselves and did the child homage. Then they opened their coffers and presented him with gifts of gold, frankincense, and myrrh. Afterward, in a dream, they received a message not to return to Herod, so they returned to their own country by another route.

The gospel of the Lord.

Chorus: Praise to you, Lord Jesus Christ.

HOMILY *(See a suggested homily in Appendix 1.)*

THE APOSTLES' CREED

Chorus: I believe in God
the Father Almighty,
Creator of heaven and earth,
and in Jesus Christ, his only Son, our Lord,
who was conceived by the Holy Spirit,
born of the Virgin Mary,
suffered under Pontius Pilate,
was crucified, died, and was buried.
He descended into hell.
On the third day he rose again from the dead;
he ascended into heaven
and is seated at the right hand of God the
Father Almighty.
From there he will come to judge the living
and the dead.
I believe in the Holy Spirit,
the Holy Catholic Church,
the communion of saints,
the forgiveness of sins,
the resurrection of the body,
and life everlasting. Amen.

Leader: In our Prayers of the Faithful, let us ask Almighty God for gentle light on those in physical, mental, or spiritual darkness. *(Feel free to create your own prayers.)*

That the Lord God would guide those who guide us: our president, legislators, judges, pastors, religious, deacons, caregivers, and teachers, let us pray to the Lord.

Chorus: Lord, hear our prayer.

Leader: That our good deeds shine like a light in the darkness, let us pray to the Lord.

Chorus: Lord, hear our prayer.

Leader: That you would lift up those in the darkness of Alzheimer's, depression, and despair, let us pray to the Lord.

Chorus: Lord, hear our prayer.

Leader: For those who have left the Church, especially our family members, that they may come back home to make it a better place, let us pray to the Lord.

Chorus: Lord, hear our prayer.

Leader: For all pilgrims, seekers, and wanderers, let us pray to the Lord.

Chorus: Lord, hear our prayer.

Leader: That you would bless those who have gifted us, even when we didn't know it, let us pray to the Lord.

Chorus: Lord, hear our prayer.

Leader: For the sick and needy of our parish and community, and for all those who have died in Christ, let us pray to the Lord.

Chorus: Lord, hear our prayer.

Leader: Here you may add your own intentions.

Leader: O God of revelation, listen to the prayers of your assembled church and grant all those things for which we cry out from the depths our being, through Christ our Lord.

Chorus: Amen.

If a priest is present, Mass continues as normal from this point. If no priest is present, proceed directly to the Our Father, prayers, sign of peace, Lamb of God, Communion, closing prayer, blessing, dismissal, and hymn sung or played. If there are no consecrated Hosts, omit Communion.

ASH WEDNESDAY

OPENING MUSIC OR HYMN

OPENING PRAYER

Celebrant: Let us begin our worship together in the name of the Father and of the Son and of the Holy Spirit.

Chorus: Amen.

Leader: Let us remember one of the earliest stories of our faith (Genesis 1:27, 3:8–19):

God created Adam and Eve in the image and likeness of Yahweh himself; in the image of God he created them. But they sinned. Soon, the man and woman heard the sound of Yahweh walking in the garden in the cool of the evening and they hid from Yahweh, but Yahweh called out, saying, "Where are you?"

Chorus: "I heard the sound of you in the garden and I was afraid, so I hid."

Leader: "Have you eaten from the tree I forbade you to eat?"

Chorus: "It was the woman you put with me; she gave me the fruit and I ate it."

Leader: Yahweh asked the woman, "What is this you have done?"

Chorus: "The serpent tempted me and I ate."

Leader: To the woman, Yahweh said, "I will multiply your pains in childbearing; you shall give birth to your children in pain." To the man, Yahweh said, "Accursed be the soil because of you. With suffering shall you get your food from it, every day of your life. It shall yield you brambles and thorns, and you shall eat wild plants. With the sweat of your brow shall you eat your bread, until you return to the soil as you were taken from it."

Chorus: And so it was: Dust we are and to dust we shall return.

Leader: A reading from the book of Joel (2:12–18):
    Yet even now, says the Lord,
    return to me with all your heart,
    with fasting, with weeping, with mourning.
    Rend your hearts, not your garments.
    Return to the Lord your God,
    for he is gracious and merciful,
    slow to anger and abounding in steadfast love.
    He will relent from punishing.
    So, blow the trumpet and sanctify a fast.
    Gather the people, bless the congregation,
    and assemble the aged, and the children,
    and even infants at the breast.
    Let the priests, the ministers of the Lord,
        weep and cry out.
    Spare your people, O Lord, and do not make
        your heritage a mockery,
    a byword among the nations.
    Then the Lord will have pity on his people.

RESPONSORIAL PSALM *(Psalm 102:1–7, 12–13)*

Leader: O Lord, hear my prayer
    and let my cry come to you.
    Hide not your face from me
    in the day of my distress.

Chorus: Incline your ear to me.
    In the day when I call, answer me speedily,
    for my days vanish like smoke
    and my bones burn like fire.

Leader: Withered and dried up is my heart.

I forget to eat my bread because of my insis-
tent sighing.
I am reduced to skin and bones.

Chorus: I am like a desert owl
among the ruins.
I am sleepless and I moan.
I am like a sparrow alone on a housetop.

Leader: But you, O Lord, abide forever
and your name endures through all generations.
You will arise and have mercy on Zion,
for it is time to pity her,
for the appointed time has come.

Leader: A reading of the Holy Gospel according to Luke (7:36–50):

At that time, one of the Pharisees named Simon asked Jesus
to dine with him. Jesus accepted and went to Simon's house
and took his place at table. Now, there was a woman—a known
sinner—who heard that Jesus was there. Unannounced, she
came into the house bearing an alabaster jar of ointment and,
weeping, began to bathe Jesus' feet with her tears, dry them
with her hair, and ended by anointing them with the ointment
she brought.

Scandalized, the Pharisee thought to himself: "Some
prophet! He should know what kind of woman this is. She's a
sinner!" His look betrayed him, so Jesus, noticing, said, "Simon,
I have a case for you. There was a certain creditor who had two
people who owned him money. One owed a great deal, the other
considerably less so. Neither could pay, so he wound up cancel-
ing both their debts. Now, which of the two will be more grateful, will love him more?"

Simon answered, "Well, I suppose, the one for whom he can-
celed the greater debt." Jesus responded, "You spoke correctly."

Then, motioning to the woman, Jesus asked, "Do you see this
woman? When I entered your house, you gave me no water for
my feet, but she has bathed my feet with her tears and dried them
with her hair. You gave me no kiss of greeting, but from the time
I came in, she has not stopped kissing my feet. You did not give

me the customary anointing of the head, but she has anointed my feet with ointment. This woman you see—yes, every bit a sinner that she is—has been forgiven, for she has shown great love."

Jesus then said to the woman, "Your sins are forgiven." At that, everyone at the table began to mumble, "Who does he think he is, that he even forgives sins?" But Jesus ignored them and simply said to the woman, "Your faith has saved you. Go in peace."

The Gospel of the Lord.

Chorus: Praise to you, Lord Jesus Christ.

HOMILY *(You may use the one in Appendix 1.)*

BLESSING OF THE ASHES

Leader: Dear friends in Christ,
Let us ask our gracious God
to bless these ashes
that we will use
as the mark of our repentance.

Lord, bless the sinner who asks for your
forgiveness
and bless + all those who receive these ashes.
May we keep this Lenten season
in preparation for the joy of Easter.
We ask this through Christ our Lord.

Chorus: Amen.

Distribute ashes (if there is any danger of spreading disease, moisten ashes and use disposable double-tipped cotton swabs to place the ashes), saying:

"Remember now that thou art dust and unto dust thou shalt return."

I prefer to keep the archaic "thou art" as a reminder of the ancientness and mystery of the event. The Church has also provided an alternative: "Repent, and believe in the Gospel," reflecting Mark 1:15.

CLOSING PRAYER

Leader: Lord, bless us who seek your forgiveness and bless all who have received these ashes. May we fervently keep this Lenten season and, by our witness, restore peace, virtue, and your Holy Presence to our troubled times. We ask this through Christ our Lord.

Chorus: Amen.

CLOSING HYMN *(optional)*

DISMISSAL

Leader: May the Lord bless and keep you,
    may the Lord let his face shine upon you
    and give you peace as you begin your Lenten
       journey.
    Our service is ended. Go in peace.

Chorus: Thanks be to God.

PASSION OR PALM SUNDAY

Leader: Dear friends in Christ, for five weeks of Lent we have been preparing, by works of charity and self-sacrifice, for the celebration of the Lord's great drama of self-giving love. Today we come together to begin this solemn week in union with the whole Church throughout the world: the free Church and the persecuted Church. Christ entered in triumph into his own city to complete his work as our Messiah: to suffer, to die, and to rise again. Let us remember with devotion this entry strewn with palms, which began his saving work, and follow him with lively faith. United with him in his suffering on the cross, may we share his resurrection and new life.

> Almighty God,
> we pray you,
> bless these palms
> and make them holy.

Today we joyfully proclaim Jesus as our Messiah and King. May we one day reach the happiness of the new and everlasting Jerusalem by faithfully following him who lives and reigns forever and ever.

Chorus: Amen.

Distribute palms.

Leader: Normally there is a homily after the Passion reading. Since the Passion is so long, I will say a few words *before* the reading, so as to set the tone. Thus:

Even for all the dangers, some people still travel to the Holy Land to trace the steps of Jesus on his way to Calvary— the route called the *Via Dolorosa*: the street full of sorrows. I want to briefly share with you one church on the pilgrimage: the Church of Saint Peter's in Gallicantu. To the locals, it has a nickname. Cunningly, they call it the Church of Saint Peter and All Cowards. The reason is that, when you step outside the church, you're standing in what once was the courtyard of the house of the high priest Caiaphas. At this place, Simon Peter, who had followed his dear friend from the Garden of Gethsemane, also found himself on trial.

The judge at this trial was not the high priest, but a common household maid and the bystanders gathered in the courtyard. There, Peter three times denied that he even knew Jesus and attempted to completely disassociate himself from the prisoner who stood before the judge inside. Peter, as we know, lied. He gave false testimony. Then, as a rooster crowed, Peter remembered the prophecy of Jesus about his cowardly betrayal and fled the courtyard, sobbing in grief.

Peter's courtyard performance happens every day, when you and I are called on to give testimony regarding our relationship to Jesus and his teachings. While we seldom verbally deny him or his way of life, we often choose an even more cowardly position: silence. While we will not be executed for witnessing to our beliefs, we fear another type of dying: the painful death of being socially scorned and rejected by our friends. So, we stand far too often with Peter and the other cowards. Too many times, by our silence or our outright agreement with evil, we deny our consciences and our Lord.

Well, today, at any rate, among friends who are here to worship with us, we can publicly proclaim, out loud, our faith in Jesus, and enter into the story of his Passion—a story that, in so many ways, is our story. So, let us begin.

(I suggest that a man take the role of narrator and a woman take the role of Christ. Here, the word "chorus" is used, rather than "crowd," because it functions like a Greek chorus in its refrain-like responses.)

Narrator: The Passion of our Lord Jesus Christ according to Matthew (26:17–27:60).

On the first day of Unleavened Bread, when it was the custom to sacrifice the paschal lamb, Jesus' disciples asked Jesus:

Chorus: Where do you wish us to go to prepare the Passover?

Narrator: Jesus instructed them,

Christ: Go into the city and you will come upon a man who will be carrying a water jar. Follow him and, in whatever house he enters, say to the owner, "The Teacher is asking, 'Where is the guest room where I may eat the Passover with my disciples?'" At that point, he will show you an upstairs room, quite spacious, furnished, and in good order. That is the place you will get ready for us.

Narrator: So, the disciples went off as they were told. When they reached Jerusalem, they found the man and the room Jesus mentioned and got ready for the Passover supper.

At dusk, Jesus arrived with the Twelve. They all reclined at table and, in the course of the meal, Jesus suddenly jarred them by saying,

Christ: Mark my word: One of you here is about to betray me; yes, one who, at this moment, is eating with me.

Narrator: They began to say to him, with alarm, one by one,

Chorus: Surely not I!

Narrator: Jesus looked at them and replied:

Christ: Yes, it is one of you here—the man who dips food into the dish with me. I tell you, the Son of Man is indeed going the way that scripture tells of him. Still, accursed be that man by whom the Son of Man is betrayed. It would be better for him had he never been born.

Narrator: There was a long silence and then, as the meal went on, Jesus took bread, blessed and broke it, and gave it to the Twelve, saying:

Christ: Take this. This is my body.

Narrator: He likewise took a cup, gave thanks, and passed it to them, and they all drank from it. He then said to them:

Christ: This is my blood, the blood of the covenant, to be poured out on behalf of many. I solemnly assure you, I will never again drink of the fruit of the vine until the day I drink it in the Reign of God.

Narrator: After singing songs of praise, they headed out for the Mount of Olives. On the way, Jesus said to them:

Christ: Your faith in me shall be shaken, but after I am raised up, I will go to Galilee ahead of you.

Narrator: Peter quickly responded,

Chorus: Even though everyone else is shaken in faith, it won't be that way with me.

Narrator: Jesus turned and looked at him and said,

Christ: Peter, let me tell you this. This very night, before the cock crows twice, you will deny me three times.

Narrator: But Peter kept hotly reassuring him, protesting,

Chorus: No, no! Even if I wind up dying with you, I will not disown you.

Narrator: The rest of the disciples all said the same thing. Jesus said nothing more. They finally came to a place called Gethsemane and Jesus said to the disciples:

Christ: Sit down here while I go and pray.

Narrator: Then he took along with him Peter, James, and John. Noticeably, he began to be filled with fear and dread. He said to the three,

Christ: My heart is heavy with sorrow to the point of death. Stay here to comfort me and keep awake.

Narrator: Then Jesus advanced a little and collapsed to the ground, praying aloud that, if it were possible, this terrible hour might pass him by. He kept saying, over and over again:

Christ: O Father, dear Abba, you have the power to do all things. So, please take this cup away from me. Still, let it be done as you would have it, not I.

Narrator: When he recovered, he returned, only to find the three disciples sound asleep. He said to Peter—reverting to his old name,

Christ: Asleep, Simon? You couldn't stay awake for even an hour? Be on guard. Pray that you will not be put to the test this way. I know the spirit is willing, but nature is weak. Stay awake in my time of need.

Narrator: Jesus went back again and once more prayed in the same mournful words. When he was done, he went back and once more found the three asleep. They could not keep their eyes open and were at a loss for words. Jesus shook his head and went back one more time. When he returned, he said to them:

Christ: Still sleeping? Still taking your ease? Well, no matter. The hour is now upon us. You will soon see the Son of Man handed over into the clutches of wicked people. So, rouse yourselves. Come along. Look, there is my betrayer.

Narrator: He had hardly finished his words when Judas appeared, surrounded by a crowd armed with swords and clubs, a crowd sent by the chief priests, scribes, and elders. Judas had arranged a signal for them, saying:

Chorus: The man I shall embrace is the one you want. Arrest him and lead him away, but be careful. He's a slippery one.

Narrator: Judas then went straightaway over to Jesus and said sweetly, "Rabbi," and embraced him. At this, the Temple guards seized Jesus and arrested him. They led Jesus to the high priest's headquarters. The crowd followed, among them Peter, who found a place by the fire outside in the courtyard. Meanwhile, the chief priests were seeking witnesses against Jesus, most of whom could not agree with one another, so the high priest himself took over. He said to Jesus:

Chorus: Have you no answer to the charges brought against you?

Narrator: Jesus remained silent, so once more the high priest said:

Chorus: Tell me outright. Are you the Messiah, the Son of the Blessed One?

Narrator: Jesus answered,

Christ: I am.

Narrator: At that, the high priest tore his robes and exclaimed,

Chorus: What more do we need? You've heard the blasphemy yourselves. What is your verdict?

Narrator: They all shouted,

Chorus: He is guilty!

Narrator: And some began to abuse him. Meanwhile, back at the courtyard, a servant girl noticed Peter warming himself at the fire and took a closer look, exclaiming,

Chorus: Why, you too were with this Jesus of Nazareth, weren't you?

Narrator: Peter quickly denied it, spitting out:

Chorus: I don't know what you're taking about. What are you trying to say?

Narrator: Peter moved from the fire toward the courtyard gate. That same suspicious servant girl followed him and yelled to the bystanders,

Chorus: Yes, this man was one of them, one of the followers of the Nazarene.

Narrator: Once again, Peter heatedly denied it. Then some of the bystanders themselves chimed in, saying to Peter:

Chorus: You *are* one of them. You're a Galilean, aren't you? Your accent gives you away.

Narrator: At that, Peter began to curse, shouting,

Chorus: I don't know what you're taking about! I don't even know the man!

Narrator: Just at that precise moment, a second cockcrow was heard and the stunned Peter recalled the prediction Jesus had made about him denying Jesus three times before the cock crowed twice. He was suddenly choked with guilt. He broke down and began to cry so vehemently and so heavily that a later legend arose that two furrows were eventually etched into his face, under his eyes, which remained there forever.

By daybreak, the chief priests, elders, and scribes had reached a decision. They bound Jesus and handed him over to the Roman governor, Pilate, since they could not impose the death penalty. Pilate asked Jesus:

Chorus: Are you the king of the Jews?

Narrator: Jesus replied,

Christ: You are the one who is saying it.

Narrator: Pilate said,

Chorus: But surely you have some kind of answer. Look at how many accusations they are leveling against you.

Narrator: But, greatly to Pilate's amazement, Jesus made no further response.

Now, on the occasion of a festival, Pilate would release for them one prisoner, anyone the crowd asked for. It so happened that there was a prisoner named Barabbas, a rebel and murderer. Pilate, who knew all along that the chief priests had handed Jesus over out of jealousy, said to the crowd:

Chorus: Do you want me to release this man, Jesus, or this murderer, Barabbas?

Narrator: Pilate was surprised that they shouted back,

Chorus: Release Barabbas!

Narrator: Pilate then asked,

Chorus: Then what am I to do with this man you call king of the Jews?

Narrator: They shouted back again,

Chorus: Crucify him!

Narrator: Stunned, Pilate asked,

Chorus: Why? What crime has he committed?

Narrator: They only shouted the louder:

Chorus: Crucify him!

Narrator: So, Pilate released Barabbas to them and, after he had Jesus scourged, he handed him over to be crucified.

The soldiers took over and led Jesus away to the barracks. There, they draped Jesus in a purple cloak, wove a crown made of thorns and pressed it on his head, and began to mock him, saying,

Chorus: All hail, king of the Jews!

Narrator: All the while, they kept striking Jesus on the head, spat at him, and bowed before him with rude laughter. When they had tired of their cruel sport, they took off the purple cloak, dressed him in his own clothes, and, forcing him to carry his own cross, led him out to crucify him.

Gradually, seeing how weak Jesus was growing and fearing he might die before crucifixion, the soldiers grabbed a farmer named Simon of Cyrene, and forced him to help carry the cross. The soldiers dragged Jesus to Golgotha's hill and crucified him there. Then they tacked up a mocking sign that read, "The King of the Jews."

They crucified him between two thieves. Soon the crowd began to hurl insults, saying,

Chorus: So! You were the one who was going to destroy the Temple and rebuild it in three days. Well, save yourself now by coming down from the cross and we'll believe you.

Narrator: And they laughed. The chief priest and scribes joined in:

Chorus: He saved others, but he can't save himself. If he's the Messiah and king of Israel, let him come down from the cross and then we'll believe in him!

Narrator: Finally, noon came and darkness fell over the whole countryside. It lasted until midafternoon. At that time, Jesus cried out in a loud voice,

Christ: My God, my God, why have you forsaken me?

Narrator: Then, uttering a final loud cry, he breathed his last and died.

(Pause for a moment in reverent reflection)

Narrator: As it grew dark—and it being the eve of the Sabbath—it was necessary for Jesus to be buried quickly. Before long, a member of the Jewish Council, Joseph from Arimathea, who was a secret seeker of truth, got up the courage to go to Pilate and ask for the body of Jesus for burial. Pilate was quite surprised that Jesus died so quickly. He called in the centurion who was in charge of the crucifixion to confirm it, then released the corpse to Joseph.

Joseph, along with some women who had followed Jesus on the way of the cross, took Jesus down, wrapped him in linen, and laid him in a tomb cut out of the rock. They then rolled a stone across the entrance. The women looked carefully in order to remember where Jesus had been laid so that they could come back after the Sabbath and anoint the dead body. Then, with heavy hearts, they returned home.

If there is no priest present, then, after the Apostles' Creed, proceed directly to the Our Father, followed by the prayers below. You may wish to conclude with an exit hymn.

Leader: Deliver us, Lord, we pray, from every evil,
      graciously grant peace in our days, so that,
      by the help of your mercy, we may always be
          free from sin
      and safe from all distress as we await the
          blessed hope
      and the coming of our Savior, Jesus Christ.

Chorus: For the kingdom, the power, and the glory are yours, now and for ever.

Leader: Lord Jesus Christ, who said to your Apostles:
      Peace I leave you, my peace I give you,
      look not on our sins, but on the faith of
          your Church,
      and graciously grant her peace and unity
      in accordance with your will,
      who live and reign for ever and ever.

Chorus: Amen.

Leader: The peace of the Lord be with you always.

Chorus: And with your spirit.

Leader: Let us offer each other the sign of peace. [*in whatever manner that might safely be.*]

Leader and Chorus:
      Lamb of God, you take away the sins of
          the world,
      have mercy on us.
      Lamb of God, you take away the sins of
          the world,
      have mercy on us.
      Lamb of God, you take away the sins of
          the world.
      grant us peace.

INVITATION TO COMMUNION

Leader: Behold the Lamb of God,
behold him who takes away the sins of the
world.
Blessed are those called to the supper of the
Lamb.

Chorus: Lord, I am not worthy that you should enter
under my roof,
but only say the word and my soul shall be
healed.

Distribution of Communion follows.

CONCLUDING RITES

Leader: The Lord be with you.

Chorus: And with your spirit.

Leader: May almighty God bless us, the Father, and the Son, +
and the Holy Spirit.

Chorus: Amen.

Leader: The Mass is ended. Go in peace.

Chorus: Thanks be to God.

✒ COMMUNAL PENITENTIAL RITE AND CONFESSION WITH GENERAL ABSOLUTION

A word on general absolution.

In 1973, following the makeover at Vatican II regarding the sacraments, Pope Paul VI issued a decree underscoring the traditional use of the sacrament of reconciliation, or penance, as it used to be called. He repeated the old five-part progression most of us learned as children (see if you remember them): (1) examine your conscience, (2) be sorry for your sins, (3) determine to try not to repeat those sins, (4) confess your sins to a priest who gives you absolution, and (5) do the penance he imposes. (How did you do?)

That's the norm and it remains as such. Nevertheless, these being the troubled times of the real world, exceptions have to be made. During times of crisis, one-to-one confession with a priest might be impossible or impracticable. Think of large emergencies like an explosion or the 9/11 tragedy or the coronavirus pandemic. Another obvious example would be a large battalion of troops suddenly being called to the front and there is only one chaplain. In these and similar cases, General Absolution may be given by a single priest without the one-on-one encounter.

Similarly, today, there is often a dearth of priests available to hear individual confessions, or there are illnesses or pandemics that make one-to-one encounters unwise, so General Absolution is called for. There is an understanding that unless circumstances prohibit it, the individual will make a one-to-one confession sometime later. In practice—for example, seniors who, in some instances, are unable to travel because of lockdown, mobility issues, or illness—the question of getting to a one-to-one confession later could be moot.

I might add that with officialdom's usual nervousness about such matters, the priest giving the General Absolution should get the bishop's permission, either before or after the circumstance. My thought is that, with Vatican II's quite generous acknowledgment of the primacy of conscience for the laity, the priest's prudential conscience judgment in this matter should be sufficient.

Anyway, be assured that the use of General Absolution is quite normal and valid here. You will receive absolution and a penance after our communal preparation of prayer, examination of conscience, and hearing of scripture. Finally, remember that this is an emergency and that, when circumstances permit, one-on-one confession is preferred. Difficult as it may sometimes be, it really is a beautiful, more hands-on meeting with Jesus' saving grace, a more personal and palatable encounter, and a means of personal growth.

So, following is the script for a penitential rite of repentance without the priest and, using the same rite, a preparation for General Absolution with a priest present.

OPENING MUSIC OR HYMN

OPENING PRAYER

Leader: Loving God of the Second Chance, here we are again, once more in need of your steadfast love. We have sinned in what we have done. We have sinned in what we have left undone. At times, we have been faithless witnesses to your justice, faded signs of your presence. We have too often let things replace people, revenge replace forgiveness, silence replace prophecy, betrayal replace fidelity, weakness replace sacrifice, and selfishness replace generosity of heart.

Our litany of sins is long. Our hope is that your mercy is longer. We are a good people, but too often led astray by the shallow allurements of this world and human respect.

But here, in this place, this time, as a people, as a gathered Church, we have come to confess our sins and restore our love for you with full confidence in your love for us.

Leader: A Reading from the Book of Nehemiah (1:1b–9a):

In the month of Kislev in the 20th year, while I was in the citadel of Susa, Hanani, one of my brothers, came from Judah with news about the survivors who witnessed the sack of Jerusalem. They related how the walls of Jerusalem were broken down, its gates burned. When I heard these things, I sat down and wept. For days, I mourned and fasted and prayed before the God of heaven.

I cried, "Lord, the great and awesome God who keeps his covenant of love with those who love him and keep his commandments, let your ear be attentive and your eyes open to hear the prayer your servant is praying. I confess the sins we Israelites have committed against you. We have acted wickedly toward you. We have not obeyed your commands, decrees, and laws you gave your servant Moses. Remember what you told him: 'If you are unfaithful, I will scatter you among the nations. But if you return to me, then even if your exiled people are on the farthest horizon, I will gather them.'"

The word of the Lord.

RESPONSORIAL PRAYER

Leader: Spirit, come transform us.
    Come, be our breath, be our hope.

Chorus: Spirit, come transform us.
    Come, be our breath, be our hope.

Leader: Deep in the womb of your presence, O God,
    Draw us to share others' burdens, healing and
        loving with truth.

Chorus: Spirit, come transform us.
    Come, be our breath, be our hope.

Leader: Open our lives to each other, show us that we
        are all one.
    You are the grace that sustains us, comforting
        spirit of God.

Chorus: Spirit, come transform us.
Come, be our breath, be our hope.

Leader: Light for our summers of wholeness, fire for
our winters of pain.
Nurturing friend, you invite us to freedom,
healing, and joy.

Chorus: Spirit, come transform us.
Come, be our breath, be our hope.

Leader: A reading of the Holy Gospel in the spirit of Luke (15:11–24):
Once upon a time, there was a father who had two sons.
One, the elder, was good, reliable, and dependable. The younger
son was good, a hard worker, but a dreamer. Some of the
migrant help used to fill the younger son's ears with stories of
life in the big city, where there were excitement, booze, and
girls for the taking. So, one day he went to his father and said
that, sooner or later, he knew his father would leave him something, so could he have it now? He wanted to leave the farm
and move to the city. The father was hurt and tried to dissuade
him, but eventually the son wore his father down and one day,
off he went.

The migrants were right: There indeed were excitement,
lights, drugs, booze, girls, and plenty of new friends. But, before
he knew it, time just whizzed by. One day, the son woke and
found he had no more money. He had blown it all. Simultane-
ously, he realized he had no more friends either. Dejected and
lonely, eventually starving and needy, he became so desperate that he, raised a faithful Jewish boy, found himself tending
pigs—despite religious injunctions against eating pork. How low
he had fallen! Many a time, he recalled his house, with the servants, a warm bed, good food, and, above all, his father, who was
forever so good to him.

One day, he made up his mind. Sorry and repentant, he
would swallow his pride and go back home. If his father would
take him back, he would no longer be his son, but a mere hired
hand. He practiced the little speech he would make when he got
there. So, off he went.

He had no idea that, all during this time, every morning before work began, his father would walk to the edge of the property and look, hoping and straining to see his son, but he never did. He would return to the house with a heavy heart. Until one day, at the edge of the property, just as the father was about to turn back, he thought he saw a figure in the distance. He watched and waited until it drew nearer. Emaciated and ragged though the figure was, the Father knew in an instant it was his son.

For a moment, a brief moment, he hesitated. Fleetingly, he thought to himself, "It's him all right. So, let the reprobate come. Let him snivel and cower before me, begging me to take him back. Not on your life. He blew it. Let him live with it." But then the father came to himself and said, "What am I thinking? What am I thinking? That's my son. That's my son! I love him!"

Then the hired help saw a remarkable thing: The father, the master, the patriarch himself ran down, puffing and huffing, till he met his son, who only got out the first word of his memorized speech—"Father"—before he was embraced by trembling arms and soaked with a million tears. When he caught his breath, the father shouted to the gawking help, "Quickly, get the fattened calf and prepare a banquet. We must celebrate, for this son of mine was dead and is now alive, was lost but now is found."

The gospel of the Lord.

Chorus: Praise to you, Lord Jesus Christ.

The following reflection may be shared.

Sin may have gotten a bad name not only because modern society has embraced a therapeutic view of the world instead of a spiritual one, but also because it became only a surface category. Older Catholics remember the examination of conscience lists they checked off before they proceeded to the five steps to making a good confession. Let's see how good your memory is. The five steps to a good confession are: examine your conscience, be sorry for your sins, have a firm purpose of amendment, confess your sins to the priest, and be willing to do the penance the priest gives you. How did you do? Examining your conscience meant running through the checklists of the three theological virtues, the four cardinal virtues, the six Commandments of the Church, the seven spiritual and corporal works of mercy, and the Ten Commandments. We were big on numbers in those days.

The problem with this was that preoccupation with the mechanics derailed any sense of what sin was really all about. It wasn't an item on a list. It was the stumbling in the ebb and flow of life. It was a detour on the way to the full love of God, an attitude, or an off-the-mark act. Indeed, the word *sin* originally meant "missing the mark." Sin is something that goes deep into the soul. It taps into the tendency we have to mess up, that tendency Christianity has called Original Sin. Sin is a pattern thing, something that pulls us down, or aside and backward. It's made up of the rhythms of our small compromises, betrayals, self-interest, pride, and omissions.

People don't realize that, which is why good people sometimes say, "I go to confession, but I don't know what to say. I don't go around killing people or mugging others or selling drugs. I lose my temper, curse sometimes, and have impure thoughts, but that's about it." But that's so anemic, and so shallow. No wonder there's no progress in the spiritual life. Sin is deeper and broader.

Sin is that which threads through us, the inner stuff that rises up and breaks out in our speech and attitudes. It's the product of our inadequacies. Sin is the code name for the protection of our egos, the broadband of our fears, jealousies, and pride. This is the kind of sin we must confess. To be more specific, we are confessing not only the sin, but sinfulness itself.

Sin, for example, is finding it hard to say "I love you" to people who need to hear this and hear it often. Sin is the failure for being sorry, truly sorry, for what I said, for what I did that was hurtful, unjust, unfair, or fraudulent. Sin is the rash judgment of this or that person whom I tore down because it was the only way I felt I could rise up. After all, if he or she goes up, I must come down, and my frail ego must rebalance that. Sin is the jealousy I feel because I have not yet discovered the serenity that comes from detachment of ego and attachment to God, and I should confess that lack. I should confess my overweening desire for recognition, status, and superiority because I have not followed Jesus and his invitation to become like little children.

I have not even come close to washing feet as he did, as I have passed up opportunities for charity. I still harbor unforgiveness, despite Jesus' telling me to love my enemies and pray for those who hate me. Sin, in other words, is failing to framework my life within the revelation of God in the life, teachings, and death of Jesus Christ. Sin is the dedicated protection of me.

Many years ago, a woman came to confession. The priest heard her come into the box, but she said nothing. After a while, he asked, "Are you there? You wish to confess?" She responded, "I need time because I have something terrible to tell." So, he waited, wondering what awful deed she had to reveal. After a long time, she cleared her throat and said, "My besetting sin is that I have made myself the center of the universe." That was probably the best confession that priest had ever heard. No checklist. No simplistic, off-the-cuff peccadillo. She went right to the heart of the matter. She confessed, not an item, but a process, a journey detoured away from full love of God and neighbor to self-centeredness, a missed mark, a failure to love as Jesus does.

Sin is real and there is a sore need to see the world in spiritual terms. Our challenge as Christians is to use Jesus as our moral slide rule, not somebody's churchy list. When we do, we will move away from our childhood trope of "I disobeyed my mother" to the adult issues of my attitude toward others and the world, my witness to that world, my obligation to improve it and my failures to do so, my subterranean lack of wholeness. Against this background, confession becomes not just a place to deposit checklist items. It is an encounter with Jesus. It is about bringing attitudes and patterns to the wonderfully merciful Lord, to the Healer of souls. It is a humble act, exposing at once my egotism and my need for redemption.

Confession becomes the place to strike our breasts and express that gospel truth as simply and sincerely as we can:

"Oh, God, be merciful to me, a sinner. I made myself the center of the universe instead of you."

A period of silence may follow the reflection.

Leader: As we prepare for the penitential rite, let us reflect on this challenge of conscience. We are called to live a virtuous life. For the most part, we do, but at times, being human, we fail. By failure, I don't mean things like feeling hurt and angry because our grownup children do not spend enough time with us, but the deeper stuff, the gospel stuff we ignore or compromise. So, let us move beyond the commandments and the usual litany of sins and look at ourselves as God's prodigal children who have sometimes strayed. Consider carefully the following questions.

Have I been faithful to my spouse? Have I watched pornography that reduces people to things, or talked the talk that lowers respect and degrades others?

Have I overindulged in alcohol or smoking, or been immoderate with my spiritual and physical health, such as watching too much TV, overeating, or not caring for my body?

Do I watch and read too much that is secular, banal, shallow, consumerist, and vulgar, that dulls spiritual growth and perception, that decreases sensitivity to the needs of others? Do I seek to grow in understanding the faith, subscribe to good spiritual reading, take an online course on theology or church matters, or read the lives of the saints?

Am I a "busybody," being unkind to a neighbor, overcritical, holding grudges, unforgiving, or judging people solely by their color, nationality, financial status, politics, or religion? Hard as it is, do I, like Jesus, ever pray for those who have hurt me, and hurt me deeply?

Have I used my physical limitations as an excuse for laziness and indifference: neglecting prayer, neglecting to vote, neglecting to reach out and help out?

Have I been unkind to callers, impatient with visitors, crabby when things didn't go my way, criticizing everybody, and seldom showing my gratitude and appreciation?

Have I practiced the virtue of humility, accepting compliments graciously, letting someone else be the center of attention, or feeling that I don't need confession or this rite because I never leave this place?

Do I try to be kind? Am I jealous of others, gossip and down-play them? Am I angry at others' good fortune? Do I fail to show gratitude to those who care for me, seldom write the occasional note to friends and benefactors and those who are sad—who, like ourselves, know what loneliness is?

Allow for a moment of silence.

Leader: Let us conclude by praying with intention the prayer the Church prays when it assembles:

Chorus: I confess to Almighty God,
      and to you, my brothers and sisters,
      that I have greatly sinned,
      in my thoughts and in my words,
      in what I have done
      and in what I have failed to do,
      through my fault, through my fault,
      through my most grievous fault.
      Therefore I ask blessed Mary ever-virgin,
      all the angels and saints,
      and you, my brothers and sisters
      to pray for me to the Lord our God.

Leader: (*making the sign of the cross*) May Almighty God have mercy on us, forgive us our sins, and bring us to life everlasting.

Chorus: Amen.

Leader: Your sins are forgiven. Go in peace.

CLOSING HYMN

Amazing grace, how sweet the sound
that saved a wretch like me.
I once was lost but now am found,
was blind but now I see.

'Twas grace that taught my heart to fear
and grace my fears relieved.
How precious did that grace appear
the hour I first believed!

With the priest present: *After the examination of conscience, all remain in silence for a few minutes. The priest then says:*

Leader: Let us now spend a few moments of silence and think of our sins, the hurtful things we've done, and the kind things we've left undone. Feel sorrow and regret especially for the one thing that bothers us. Concentrate on any especial harm, any serious sin that needs to be brought to the mercy of God. Be contrite.

After some time, the priest directs:

Leader: Let us pray together our Act of Contrition:

Chorus: My God,
    I am sorry for my sins with all my heart.
    In choosing to do wrong
    and failing to do good,
    I have sinned against you
    whom I should love above all things.
    I firmly intend, with your help,
    to do penance,
    to sin no more,
    and to avoid whatever leads me to sin.
    Our Savior Jesus Christ suffered and died for us.
    In his name, my God, have mercy.

The priest offers some penance and then gives Absolution. As he extends his hands (or right hand) over the assembled penitents, he says:

Leader: God, the Father of mercies,
    through the death and resurrection of his Son
    has reconciled the world to himself
    and sent the Holy Spirit among us for the forgiveness of sins;
    through the ministry of the Church, may God give you pardon and peace,
    and I absolve you from your sins
    in the name of the Father + and of the Son,
    and of the Holy Spirit.

Chorus: Amen.

Leader: Your sins are forgiven. Go in peace.

Chorus: Thanks be to God.

CLOSING HYMN *(see above)*

A HOLY THURSDAY LITURGY

There are two parts here. Part I includes the liturgy up to the point of Communion (with directions for when no priest is present) and Part II includes Mass if a priest is present. The first part is not official and offers more flexibility as to time and place. It's conceivable that the parish priest can celebrate the official liturgy at one time in church and perhaps let others offer the unofficial liturgy at another church he can't get to. Part I is quite moving and especially convenient for situations outside the parish setting.

For context, the church is in semi-darkness. The Twelve Disciples, six males and six females, ranging from ages 8 to 80, are dressed in white robes (made by the people). They enter and process silently in single file down the aisle, carrying lighted candles. They ascend a small platform erected in front of the altar. The leader goes to the pulpit and the "Christ" to another lectern. All sit (and the Disciples extinguish their candles). The conversation below begins. The people, of course, have this booklet with the full service in it.

When the washing of the feet is over (done to some lovely background music) and this part of the service is over, the Twelve Disciples join the priest (or leader) at the altar, six on either side, for the Mass or Communion Service. At Communion time, each person may be given a lighted candle as he or she departs after receiving. (For those nervous about a fire hazard, use battery-powered candles.) At the end of the liturgy, the priest strips the altar, giving each article to one of the Disciples who, holding it high, walks down the center aisle to the sacristy. The lights in church are gradually extinguished during this process, till only candlelight prevails. After the altar is stripped, the priest or leader leaves silently down the center aisle and the liturgy is over. The lights go up to semi-darkness and the people depart.

If this Holy Thursday service takes place outside the parish church, accommodations may be made. At senior residences, I suggest no platform, no robes, and maybe only one or two token Disciples whose feet are washed.

I. LITURGY PRECEDING COMMUNION
(without a Priest)

Leader: Good Evening. Tonight, we do not celebrate like other nights. Tonight is a very special night. Tonight, we tell stories and wash feet and break bread and share a cup. We have done these things before, but tonight they have a deeper meaning, because it is the time of Passover and all is ready for the feast.

Let us begin our story as, for centuries, in the land of Israel, in countless Jewish homes, as the sun began to set, families would gather together to celebrate a special meal. And the youngest member of the family would ask these age-old questions:

Chorus: Why is this night different from other nights? Why is this meal special?

Leader: This night is the Passover of the Lord. On this night, the Lord passed over the land of Egypt. He struck down the firstborn of the Egyptians, but spared the children of Israel. On that night, we ate in haste, for we were to flee at the word of the Lord. The Lord was saving us from the slavery of Egypt. He was leading us forth with a mighty hand and outstretched arm. The Lord was a cloud by day and a column of fire by night. He drowned our foes in the Red Sea while we passed safely through the waters. The Lord led us through the desert to the mountain of Sinai. There, He entered into a covenant with us. He became our God and we became His people.

Chorus: A wonderful bond! What else did the Lord do?

Leader: Much more. The Lord gave us a Law we should observe and vowed to lead us to the Promised Land. For forty years in the desert, He gave us Manna to eat and water from the rock to drink. Finally, He led us into the land of Canaan, gave us victory over our enemies, and gave us this land as our own. And so we celebrate the Passover meal tonight because it is the night the Lord delivered us from prison and made us a free people.

Chorus: But surely there is more to tell. Why is this night different for those who follow the Way, and the one called Jesus?

Leader: Let us go back over nineteen hundred years. The scene is in an eastern city called Jerusalem. It is crowded with pilgrims because these are the days of Passover. Among them are a group of poor men, mostly fishermen, with the rough accents of Galilee. They have a leader called Jesus, the son of a carpenter from Nazareth.

Earlier in the day, Jesus had sent two of them, Peter and John, to prepare a meal. They purchased a lamb, had it ritually slaughtered in the Temple, and bought wild herbs and lettuce, unleavened bread and wine, for these were the traditional foods of the Passover. The Upper Room was ready, the couches were drawn around the table. They came in, weary from the road. There was some jostling for the best places but, finally, all was ready and their leader spoke to them:

Christ: I have longed to eat this Passover with you before I suffer, because I tell you that I shall not eat it again until it is fulfilled in the Reign of God.

Leader: And so they ate the Passover meal.

Chorus: But why do *we* eat of the one bread tonight?

Leader: Do you not know what Jesus did on this night? He took the bread and, after he had given thanks, he broke it, and gave it to them, saying:

Christ: Take this, all of you, and eat it. This is my body, which shall be given up for you.

Leader: And so, the bread that we break is communion in the body of Christ. The fact that there is one bread means that, though there are many of us, we form a single body—all of us who share in the one bread.

Chorus: And why do we drink of the fruit of the vine tonight?

Leader: Because on that night, at the end of the meal, Jesus took the cup of blessing, gave praise and thanks, and gave it to his disciples, saying:

Christ: Take this, all of you, and drink of it, for this cup is the new covenant, the promise that I seal with my blood. Do this, whenever you drink it, to remember that I live in your midst. I tell you, I shall not drink of the fruit of the vine again until the day I drink it anew in the Reign of God.

Leader: And so, this Blessing Cup that we bless is a communion with the blood of Christ. And every time we eat this bread and drink this cup, we proclaim that Jesus went through death to life. He is Lord and comes in the midst of us.

Chorus: But one last question. Why do we wash feet tonight?

Leader: Because Jesus knew that the hour had come for him to pass from this world to the Father. He had preached a new commandment of love and now he would show his love in action. They called him "Master," but he said:

Christ: I am in the midst of you as one who serves.

Leader: Then he rose up from the meal, took off his cloak, and wrapped a towel around himself. He picked up a basin and began to wash his disciples' feet and to dry them with the towel. He came to Simon Peter, who asked:

Chorus: Lord, are you going to wash my feet?

Christ: You may not realize now what I am doing, but later you will understand.

Chorus: You will I never wash my feet!

Christ: If I do not wash you, you will have no share in my heritage.

Chorus: Then, Lord, wash not only my feet, but my hands and head as well.

Christ: The one who has bathed has no need to wash, except for his feet. He is entirely cleansed, just as you are.

Leader: And so, he washed the feet of his disciples.

If there is to be a washing of the feet, I suggest a symbolic act involving no more than four people. When the washing is done, the dialogue concludes:

Christ: Do you understand what I just did for you? You address me as Teacher and Lord, and fittingly so, for that is what I am. But if I who am Teacher and Lord have washed your feet, then you must wash each other's feet. What I just did was to give you an example. As I have done, so you must do.

All: This is the Gospel, the Good News of the Lord.

Here follows a brief reflection, or you may use the longer, more vivid homily in Appendix 1.

"Do you understand what I have done?" Jesus asked when he was finally finished washing feet and straightened up. Not really. The disciples did not understand at the time. It took time for the message to sink in. It took time to appreciate the love that was freely and equally given to sinner and saint—and that, in fact, the Master would repeat this washing, this loving, time and time again, till time ran out.

For there would be a modern-day Peter, one with great power in the church; one, alas, with blindness in his heart to what was around him: the poverty, the injustice, the murders of innocent people. Then, one quiet day, Jesus Christ took up his towel and basin once again and washed this prelate's feet and Archbishop Óscar Romero of El Salvador came out of the shadows to embrace his people and openly spoke out against an evil regime. On another day, standing at the Eucharist, he heard a rifle shot fired by that same evil regime, and he died at the altar, mingling his blood with the blood of Christ.

There was a zealot too: a woman of communist leanings and bohemian ways, with her live-in boyfriend and illegitimate child. But Jesus Christ stalked her and sought her out, and he washed her feet and took away her sins, and made this woman, Dorothy Day, hot for justice—this woman, this apostle of the poor, whose cause is now up for canonization.

This modern-day doubter was reluctant. Saucy and intellectual, too bright to believe, an unwed father, a gadfly of the books and colleges like Columbia University, which he attended. But, eventually, Jesus caught up with him, sat him down, and washed those feet with great love—and, like his namesake, Thomas Merton surrendered to it and became a convert, a monk, and a mystic.

This tax collector, unlike Matthew, walked the corridors of power. He sat at the right hand of presidential power, and he connived and plotted and bled his own people. But Jesus patiently, slowly uncovered his feet and washed them, and Charles Colson, the most powerful man in the nation next to Richard Nixon, found himself in jail—and from there, a willing prisoner of the Lord who ministered in his name for the rest of his life.

This is one traitor who didn't get away. Oh, he denied everything, with his sharp wit and sophisticated pen. He mocked religion, laughed at the Catholic Church, and got others to laugh with him—that is, till *his* proud feet were washed by a humble Jesus and Malcolm Muggeridge—playboy, wit, editor of the famed *Punch* magazine—found himself a new man and an apostle for Christ, a convert to Catholicism.

That's what time has taught. What happened on that first Holy Thursday night, which we are commemorating, was a summary of Jesus' whole mission. Throughout the ages, he would love without condition and wash the feet of all—Peter's and Óscar's, Dorothy's and Thomas', yours and mine—without regard to position, prestige, or power; without regard to shame or sorrow or sin. All would be embraced, all would be cleansed, if we would but let him.

This is what we are praying for today: that we surrender our feet to Jesus.

After the reflection, if no priest is present, move directly to your own Prayers of the Faithful, followed by the usual Communion Service procedure as outlined above.

II. HOLY THURSDAY WITH A PRIEST

If a priest is present, the Mass continues. Also, since this is the night when the Church celebrates the institution of the priesthood, it is the custom for the priest to renew his vows. After the people have recited, "Lord I am not worthy" and immediately before the priest receives Communion, a lay representative stands up from the congregation (if appropriate, the president of the Parish Council) and begins the following dialogue:

Lay Representative: Since this evening marks not only the institution of the Most Blessed Sacrament but also the beginning of that priesthood which presides over the Christian community and its Eucharist, I, on behalf of the people of God, respectfully request a statement of rededication from our pastor, Father ___.

Do you reaffirm your faith leadership of this community and its Eucharistic celebrations—in short, your priesthood—before your people?

Celebrant: I do.

Lay Representative: Do you renew your vow of celibacy, which urges you to the service of all: that, being no one's father, you are father to all; that, being no one's spouse, you are spouse to all; that, having no family of your own, everyone has a claim on you?

Celebrant: I do.

Lay Representative: Do you re-pledge yourself to the faith community of [*name of residence home/gathering/parish*] and renew your fidelity to its spiritual welfare?

Celebrant: I do.

Lay Representative: Do you wish to make your own statement of rededication, both to your priesthood and to this community?

Celebrant: I do.

Before God in heaven and before you, this Christian community, I reaffirm my priesthood. It is something that means more to me than life itself. It is a source of profound happiness and fulfillment. It is a precious and at times a difficult pilgrimage, but one that is supported by the Spirit and by my fellow travelers. I recognize that my priesthood must be in harmony with the gifts of all of you who have been given the Spirit in baptism; that my priesthood has meaning only in terms of all the people, in terms of "washing the feet of all."

Therefore, I willingly and happily restate my intention and commitment to God's work. I once more humbly give myself over to the Spirit, who alone can absorb my weaknesses and bring goodness out of human limitation.

I renew my vows of celibacy and obedience. I renew my public life for the priesthood and God's fragile Church. I renew my dedication to this community for another year.

And I pray, as always, that my sins will not hinder God's work, nor my human foibles frustrate God's designs. And I continue my deep and abiding gratitude to the people who have been, and continue to be, a never-failing source of encouragement and strength—indeed, a true and beautiful family—to me. I proclaim my words tonight under the Spirit and with the Son in the unity of the everlasting and ever-loving Father. Amen.

The Celebrant now receives Communion and Mass continues as usual.

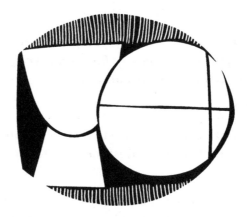

GOOD FRIDAY STATIONS OF THE CROSS

A favorite pilgrimage destination for medieval Europeans was the Holy Land. People wanted to visit the very spots Jesus walked, especially his torturous way to Calvary. But it was far away, across the waters, and many people were unable to make such a long, arduous, and often dangerous journey. So, artists among the pilgrims who did go began to sketch those Holy Land sites associated with Jesus' passion and death, usually under the care of the Franciscans who would bring them safely back to Europe. They would hang these pictures along roadsides and eventually inside churches. The number of such pictures varied from seven to twenty-four, but eventually settled at fourteen, to become our standard fourteen Stations of the Cross today.

It was important then, as it is important now, to understand the "rules" of these Stations. The fourteen stations are just that: stations or *stationary standing places*. The pilgrim of yesterday and today is to stand before the depiction of Jesus' way to the cross for two reasons. One is to meditate on the scene before you, but the other, far more important reason, is to enter into it. That is, to be a participant, to take on the role of some character in the scene: maybe a bystander, one of the crowd, the weeping women, Simon of Cyrene, one of the thieves alongside Jesus, and so on. Allow yourself to be pulled into the event and, above all, focus on the determined and emptying love of Jesus.

I have replaced the official Good Friday service with these Stations because the service is basically a Communion Service (the one day of the liturgical year when Mass is not celebrated) plus Good Friday readings and the veneration of the Cross. Formerly, for the veneration, people would line up in two rows, as though they were approaching the altar for Communion. They would advance toward a large crucifix resting on a pillow, get down on their knees, and bend over to kiss the cross. Attendants used a small cloth to wipe off the cross each time. Later, the kiss was replaced by touching the crucifix. During these days of pandemic sensitivity, neither act of veneration is advisable or feasible. People may wish instead to view a strategically placed crucifix and perhaps say some common prayers.

So, feel free to use the official rite. It's easy to assemble. Still, I suggest substituting the Stations of the Cross at 3:00 p.m. and a communal reading of the Passion (taken from Palm Sunday; see above) at 7:00 in the evening.

This version of the Stations of the Cross was originally designed to take place outdoors. My former parish of St. Mary's had a large property and I asked fifteen families, given a blueprint, to construct the crosses and erect them on the grounds—the fifteenth being draped in a white cloth. All participants had a small booklet containing the following liturgy, so they could pray and sing their parts. Usually, from 1100–1200 people attended, joined by a fair number of Protestants, including ministers. It was very moving.

If outdoors is not feasible, use the parish church or whatever space is available. In the parish church, there is a cross-bearer flanked by two acolytes who move from station to station as the narrator leads the service for the people in the pews. There is no doubt that without the rhythms of song and pilgrimage-like movement outside, something is lost indoors. This is even more so in senior residences, where participants will not be expected to move around (and often cannot do so without assistance), so I suggest you create a slide show picture for each station. The song interludes are traditionally used during transition time from one station to the next, so these can be ignored, become silent prayers, or the tunes can be simply played to set the mood if you have a musician present.

SONG: Were you there when they crucified my Lord?
Were you there when they crucified my Lord?
Oh, sometimes it causes me to tremble, tremble, tremble.
Were you there when they crucified my Lord?

THE FIRST STATION:
Jesus is unjustly accused by Pilate

Chorus: My people, what have I done to you? How have I offended you? Answer me!

Leader: I came to speak the truth, but you would not hear it.

Chorus: My people, what have I done to you? How have I offended you? Answer me!

Leader: Lord, there you are, the innocent lamb being led to slaughter, victim of misunderstanding, hatred, and the jealously of others. You weren't the first or the last.

Chorus: Brother Jesus, like you, we have experienced times in our lives when we too were falsely accused, falsely judged; when lying rumors were spread about us; when we were the victims of false gossip and false accusations. We think of the Catholic bishops in Chinese prisons accused of being spies for America, of people like St. Thomas More being sent to their deaths on trumped-up charges. If we've been unjustly accused by gossip, innuendo, or lies, how do we act? Can we identify with Jesus standing before Pilate, being silent, not returning evil for evil, believing that God will have the last word?

Leader: Lord, be with us in our trials.

Chorus: Help us to return good for evil.

SONG: Blessed are those who hunger and thirst for justice.
They will be satisfied.
Bless us, O Lord, hear our cry for justice.
Bless us, O Lord, our God.

THE SECOND STATION:
Jesus accepts his cross

Chorus: My people, what have I done to you? How have I offended you? Answer me!

Leader: I healed you of your disease and sickness and you have given me gall to drink.

Chorus: My people, what have I done to you? How have I offended you? Answer me!

Leader: Lord, you have been handed your cross. Your cross! As if it were your cross! You had no cross, and you came to take ours. Throughout your life and all during the way to Calvary, you took upon yourself our infirmities. The cross must be carried.

Chorus: Brother Jesus, I would rather fight the cross than bear it. It is too hard. The older I get and the more I see suffering in the world, the heavier is the cross on my shoulders. Help me to understand that all these sufferings, and especially my own, are but an extension of your cross. They, too, are redemptive.

Leader: Lord, you promise life in all its fullness.

Chorus: Cure us of our sicknesses.

SONG: Blessed are they who show others mercy.
They will know mercy too.
O Lord, hear our cry for mercy.
Bless us, O Lord, our God.

THE THIRD STATION:
Jesus falls the first time

Chorus: My people, what have I done to you? How have I offended you? Answer me!

Leader: I led you from slavery to freedom and you have sold yourselves into slavery again.

Chorus: My people what have I done to you? How have I offended you? Answer me!

Leader: Lord, you came to carry the burden of the cross so that my burden would be yours, but I preferred to go it alone.

Chorus: Brother Jesus, as I look around, there are so many people hurting, people with cold hearts, people weary of life, pandemics, and broken institutions. People are disillusioned by false promises, anarchy in their hearts and in the streets. They are burdened with anxieties about the future, crushed by indifference, without a sense of hope. They are fallen. Lord, lift up my spirit. Help me, Lord, when I fall.

Leader: Lord, you offered us freedom.

Chorus: Deliver us from our fears. Help us to get up again.

SONG: Sing of Mary, pure and lowly,
Virgin Mother undefiled.
Sing of God's own Son most holy,
who became her little child.
Fairest child of fairest mother,
God the Lord who came to earth,
Word made flesh, our very brother,
took our nature by his birth.

THE FOURTH STATION:
Jesus meets his mother

Chorus: My people, what have I done to you? How have I offended you? Answer me!

Leader: I offered you the example of my mother, but you have not embraced her.

Chorus: My people, what have I done to you? How have I offended you? Answer me!

Leader: Lord, your mother's heart was broken, not only because she saw you publicly disgraced and humiliated, going to your death as a common criminal, but because she could not help you. How gladly would she have changed places with you, but she was restrained by the rough soldiers.

Chorus: Brother Jesus, how clearly we see that your mother becomes every parent unable to save their children, every parent who watches by the hospital bed, every parent who has buried a child, every parent who stands by helplessly to watch a child disintegrate with drugs or alcoholism, whose marriage is falling apart. She is everyone who wants so desperately to save a loved one but can't, at least not right now.

Leader: Lord, sustain us that we may sustain others.

Chorus: May our tears join those of all who weep.

SONG: Whatsoever you do to the least of my brethren,
that you do unto me.
When I was weary, you helped me find rest.
When I was anxious, you calmed my fears.
Now enter into the home of my Father.

THE FIFTH STATION:
Simon is forced to carry Jesus' cross

Chorus: My people, what have I done to you? How have I offended you? Answer me!

Leader: I taught you to care for your brother and sister and yet you watch me suffer with unconcern.

Chorus: My people, what have I done to you? How have I offended you? Answer me!

Leader: Lord, Simon is the paradigm of all those who carry crosses they did not want or ask for or bargain for. Nobody wanted a sick parent, a child with disabilities, the cancer, the addiction, the divorce, the job loss, the depression—unwanted crosses of all descriptions.

Chorus: Brother Jesus, many of us have played the role of Simon of Cyrene. We are angry at God and frustrated. But the longer we stand here, the more we absorb the tradition that says that if Simon started out with anger, after a while of carrying it with Jesus, he moved to understanding, and from understanding he moved to love, and from love he moved on to his own salvation and became, as it were, a co-redeemer with Jesus.

Leader: The world needs Simons of Cyrene.

Chorus: Help us to help others.

SONG: O sacred head surrounded by crown of piercing thorn!
O bleeding head so wounded, reviled and put to scorn.
Death's pallid hue comes o'er thee, the glow of life decays,
yet angel hosts adore thee and tremble as they gaze.

THE SIXTH STATION:
Veronica wipes the face of Jesus

Chorus: My people, what have I done to you? How have I offended you? Answer me!

Leader: When I was disfigured, you looked the other way.

Chorus: My people, what have I done to you? How have I offended you? Answer me!

Leader: Lord, you have imprinted your image on the veil of this woman, Veronica, just as the Father imprinted your image on all of creation. But the image on this veil is bloody and disfigured. It has been marred by disrespect.

Chorus: Brother Jesus, our whole world bears the stamp of your loving creation. Yet how often have we marred or scarred that image, defaced the earth, polluted your skies, destroyed your forests, and fouled your air—all the things you gave us for our use and enjoyment. Lord, help us to restore your image once again to our planet.

Leader: You renewed all of creation.

Chorus: Take away our tendency to deface what you have redeemed.

SONG: I see thy strength and vigor all fading in the strife,
and death with cruel rigor bereaving thee of life!
O agony and dying, O love to sinners free.
Jesus, all grace supplying, O turn thy face on me.

THE SEVENTH STATION:
Jesus falls the second time

Chorus: My people, what have I done to you? How have I offended you? Answer me!

Leader: I showed you how to love and to share and you ignored me in my hour of need.

Chorus: My people, what have I done to you? How have I offended you? Answer me!

Leader: Lord, how alone you must have felt as you fell for the second time. You are exhausted and there is no one to help you up. Like a stranger in a foreign land, you are all alone. How frightening it is to suffer the pain of aloneness.

Chorus: Brother Jesus, you came to make all people one family, to unlock the beauty within each one's soul, to set it free. Lord, let me recognize the isolation of others, especially those where I live. Let me help them to know that there is someone who cares.

Leader: You promised, Lord, to be with us always.

Chorus: Rescue us from our selfish isolation.

SONG: In this thy bitter passion, Good Shepherd, think of me
with thy most sweet compassion, unworthy though I be.
Beneath thy cross abiding, forever would I rest.
In thy dear love confiding and with thy presence blest.

THE EIGHTH STATION:
Jesus speaks to the women

Chorus: My people, what have I done to you? How have I offended you? Answer me!

Leader: I came to make you one people and you have mocked me and called me names.

Chorus: My people, what have I done to you? How have I offended you? Answer me!

Leader: Lord, you spoke to the women and children, the fringe of society. Even amid your own pain, you were not just concerned with your own suffering. You took time to acknowledge these invisible people with love and understanding. You recognized them as also beloved of your Father.

Chorus: Brother Jesus, how self-absorbed I can be. How often my prejudice and my spiritual blindness keep me from seeing you in all people. I too easily dismiss the people you love so much. Lord, help me escape from my spiritual blindness.

Leader: Lord, you are all things to all people.

Chorus: Give us your way of seeing.

SONG: Bless those who suffer from persecution.
Theirs is the kingdom of God.
Bless us, O Lord, when they persecute us.
Bless us, O Lord, our God.

THE NINTH STATION:
Jesus falls the third time

Chorus: My people, what have I done to you? How have I offended you? Answer me!

Leader: I have promised to be with you, and you have not called upon me.

Chorus: My people, what have I done to you? How have I offended you? Answer me!

Leader: Lord, you struggled to get up the last time. It's only a little farther and you have fallen again onto the dusty road, again with the sound of mocking voices in your ears. How long will it be, Lord, before you have no strength to continue? Lord, for the third time, you fall—this time, close to the end.

Chorus: Brother Jesus, how many times have I promised you never to fall again? I've said it, Lord, but then I flirt with temptation, go where I should not, and fall. Lord, give me the courage always to get up and try again, one day at a time.

Leader: Lord, you strengthen us with your grace.

Chorus: Take away our weaknesses and make us strong in you.

SONG: Whatsoever you do to the least of my brethren,
that you do unto me.
When I was homeless, you opened your door.
When I was naked, you gave me your coat.
Now enter into the home of my Father.

THE TENTH STATION:
Jesus is stripped of his garments

Chorus: My people, what have I done to you? How have I offended you? Answer me!

Leader: I made you children of my Father and you have stripped me of my dignity.

Chorus: My people, what have I done to you? How have I offended you? Answer me!

Leader: Lord, you had nothing left but your own cloak. You were fond of it because your mother had woven it. But this too had to go. One thing only is needful now: your cross. Nothing can come between you and the cross. With it, you will save the world.

Chorus: Brother Jesus, we are living in a sensual and secular world. To believe the advertisements, everything stands or falls with power, accumulation, and image, not love and humble service. Why do I continue to believe that the promises of this world will save me? Lord, strip me of all systems that merely exploit so that I can see that you alone are savior.

Leader: Lord, you took upon yourself our human nature.

Chorus: Open our eyes to the needs of people and the beauty of your presence.

SONG: Were you there when they nailed him to the tree?
Were you there when they nailed him to the tree?
Oh, sometimes it causes me to tremble, tremble, tremble.
Were you there when they nailed him to the tree?

THE ELEVENTH STATION:
Jesus is nailed to the cross

Chorus: My people, what have I done to you? How have I offended you? Answer me!

Leader: With great love I have lifted you up and you have nailed me upon this tree.

Chorus: My people, what have I done to you? How have I offended you? Answer me!

Leader: Lord, you know what it means to suffer pain. As the nails are driven through your hands and feet, you cry out in weakness because life is flowing out of every pore. First, the humiliation of being beaten on your head and face, and now those terrible, sharp nails in your flesh!

Chorus: Brother Jesus, my distractions and my selfishness nail you each day in the form of my brothers and sisters. Those in mental hospitals, in jails, in tents, in orphanages, and in the streets are nailed there in pain because of our neglect. We have walled them into places where they will not disturb our consciences. Lord, disturb my comfort so that I might comfort the disturbed.

Leader: Lord, you taught us to love one another.

Chorus: Purify us of our narrow vision.

SONG: Blessed are they who mourn and sorrow.
They will be comforted.
Bless us, O Lord, when we share their sorrow.
Bless us, O Lord, our God.

THE TWELFTH STATION:
Jesus dies on the cross

Chorus: My people, what have I done to you? How have I offended you? Answer me!

Leader: I came to give you new life and you stood there and watched me die.

Chorus: My people, what have I done to you? How have I offended you? Answer me!

Leader: Lord, your death came slowly—three hours of agony—and now it is finished. You died that we might have life and have it more abundantly. You have given your last breath for all of us. What greater sign could you give us of your never-ending love?

Chorus: Brother Jesus, how many times have you died in those countless deaths that are a continuing witness of our inhumanity to one another—deaths caused by careless driving, overdose, murders, torture, neglect, senseless wars, late-term abortions. Lord, give me a profound respect for human life. Give me a dedication to the cause of preserving life and helping others to come to a fuller enjoyment of it.

Leader: Lord, you promised life forever.

Chorus: Help us to share life in all its fullness.

SONG: Forgive we now each other's faults as we our faults confess,
and let us love each other well in Christian holiness.
Let strife among us be unknown. Let all contentions cease.
Be his the glory that we seek. Be ours his holy peace.

THE THIRTEENTH STATION:
Jesus is taken down from the cross

Chorus: My people, what have I done to you? How have I offended you? Answer me!

Leader: I came to free you from loneliness and you have left me alone to die.

Chorus: My people, what have I done to you? How have I offended you? Answer me!

Leader: Lord, your work is done. You can leave your cross. Your mother takes you into her arms. You rest in peace. Alone in all the world, she holds you close.

Chorus: Brother Jesus, loneliness often forces me to question the meaning of my life, the meaning of my death. Lord, take me in your arms and hold me close. Help me to understand that you are present when I am lonely. Help me to remember the vast Communion of Saints to which I belong, who are my family.

Leader: Lord, you promised peace to all.

Chorus: Keep us from loneliness. Keep us close to you.

SONG: Were you there when they laid him in the tomb?
Were you there when they laid him in the tomb?
Oh, sometimes it causes me to tremble, tremble, tremble.
Were you there when they laid him in the tomb?

THE FOURTEENTH STATION:
Jesus is laid in the tomb

Chorus: My people, what have I done to you? How have I offended you? Answer me!

Leader: I showed you the way to the Father and you have abandoned me to a stranger's grave.

Chorus: My people, what have I done to you? How have I offended you? Answer me!

Leader: Lord, your friends have laid you to rest. The stone is set in place. It separates you from your mother, from your disciples, from your friends, from all the living. Sadness, emptiness, and isolation cause them to feel that painful anguish of separation.

Chorus: Brother Jesus, how easy it is to forget that you are alive, not dead and buried. How convenient it becomes to leave you there in the tomb, separated from my life. Help me to resurrect you in my life. Make your presence a living one. Do not allow me to isolate you to a tabernacle, a church, a creed, a book, a memory. Keep your risen presence alive in me daily as I live my life united with you.

Leader: Lord, your death brought life to the world.

Chorus: Do not separate us from your new life.

SONG: Crown him with many crowns, God's lamb upon the throne,
our debt to God which had no bounds the Lamb has made his own.
Now Christians praises sing, his death he gave for you,
acclaim the victim as your king, God's life is yours anew.

THE FIFTEENTH STATION:
Jesus is raised from the dead

Chorus: My people, what have I done to you? How have I offended you? Answer me!

Leader: I came to give you hope and you have chosen despair.

Chorus: My people, what have I done to you? How have I offended you? Answer me!

Leader: Lord, all have left you, silently slipping away, leaving you in the tomb. They leave without hope, to go home to weep and despair. They feel that all is over, that there is no redemption, no way to live again in your absence.

Chorus: Brother Jesus, how often we have felt like these people: hopeless, resigned to loss, hurt, and in pain. How often we have given up. But your resurrection teaches us that we can begin all over again, that our sins can be forgiven, that, in you, we can rise up to newness of life. Jesus, you are truly our hope.

Leader: Your resurrection is our resurrection.

Chorus: Deliver us from despair.

All: Look down upon me, good and gentle Jesus, while, before your face, I humbly kneel and, with burning soul, pray and beseech you to fix deep in my heart lively sentiments of faith, hope, and charity, true contrition for my sins, and a firm purpose of amendment of life while I contemplate with great love and tender pity your five wounds, pondering over them within me, calling to mind the words that David, your prophet, said of you, "They have pierced my hands and my feet; they have numbered all my bones." (*Psalm 22:17–18*)

(Note: If you desire to read the Passion at another time on Good Friday, refer to the Palm Sunday version. However, I don't recommend reading the Passion along with the Stations. Keep a singular focus.)

EASTER SUNDAY

No leader is going to try to do the Easter Vigil which, in the best of times, though beautiful with its singing of the Easter Proclamation and multiple readings, is too long. The Easter Vigil is also the time when converts are received into the Church. So, we skip to the Mass at daytime. Again, if there is a priest present, then the Mass goes as normally. This liturgy presumes the absence of a priest.

OPENING HYMN *(sung or played)*

Alleluia! Alleluia!
Let the holy anthem rise
and the choirs of heaven
chant it in the temple of the skies.
Let the mountains skip with gladness
and the joyful valleys ring
with hosannas in the highest
To our Savior and our King!

Leader: On this, the Church's greatest feast, let us pray:
Gracious God,
by raising Christ your Son,
you conquered the power of death
and opened for us the way to eternal life.
Let our celebration today
raise us up and renew our lives
in the Spirit that is within us.
We ask this through Christ your Son. Amen.

Leader: A reading from the Acts of the Apostles (10:34a, 37–43):
Peter addressed the people, saying, "I take it that you know by now what has been talked about all over Judea, about Jesus of Nazareth, who came from Galilee, where John baptized him and God anointed him with the Holy Spirit and power. This

Jesus went about doing good works and healing all who were in the grip of the devil. God was with him. We ourselves are witnesses to all that he did in the land of the Jews and in Jerusalem itself. You know that there they killed him, hanging him on the tree of the cross, only to have God raise him up on the third day. God allowed him to be seen, not by all, but by such witnesses as had been chosen beforehand by God—and by us, the very ones who ate with him and drank with him after he rose from the dead. This Jesus commissioned us to preach to the people and to be a witness that he indeed is the one set apart by God as judge of the living and the dead. To him all the prophets testify, saying that everyone who believes in him has forgiveness of sins through his name."

The word of the Lord.

Chorus: Thanks be to God.

RESPONSORIAL PSALM
(Psalm 118:1–2, 16–17, 22–23)

Leader: This is the day the Lord has made; let us rejoice and be glad.

Chorus: This is the day the Lord has made; let us rejoice and be glad.

Leader: Give thanks to the Lord, for he is good;
for his mercy endures forever.
Let the house of Israel say, "His mercy
endures forever."

Chorus: This is the day the Lord has made; let us rejoice and be glad.

Leader: The right hand of the Lord has struck
with power.
The right hand of the Lord is exalted.
I shall not die but live,
and declare the works of the Lord.

Chorus: This is the day the Lord has made; let us rejoice and be glad.

Leader: The stone which the builders rejected
　　　　has become the cornerstone.
　　　　By the Lord has this been done;
　　　　it is wonderful in our eyes.

Chorus: This is the day the Lord has made; Let us rejoice and be glad.

Leader: Alleluia! Christ has become our sacrifice. Let us feast with joy in the Lord.

Chorus: Alleluia!

Leader: A reading of the Holy Gospel according to John (20:1–8):
　　　Early in the morning on the first day of the week, while it was still dark outside, Mary Magdalene came to the tomb of Jesus. She saw right away that the stone had been moved away. Perplexed, she ran off to Simon Peter and the disciple whom Jesus loved and told them,

Chorus: "The Lord has been taken from the tomb! We don't know where they have put him."

Leader: At that, Peter and the other disciple ran to the tomb, side by side. The younger disciple outran Peter and reached the tomb first, but he did not enter. Rather, he bent down to peer in. What he saw were wrappings lying on the ground. Simon Peter came running up behind him and he entered the tomb. He also saw the wrappings on the ground, and also the piece of cloth that had covered Jesus' head, not lying with the wrappings, but rolled up in a place by itself. Then the other disciple went in. He too saw, and believed.
　　　The gospel of the Lord.

Chorus: Praise to you, Lord Jesus Christ.

REFLECTION *(Any reflection will do, but I offer a timely homily in Appendix 1.)*

The reflection or homily is followed by a renewal of baptismal vows.

Leader: Dear Friends, we have been buried with Christ in baptism so that we may rise with him to a new life. Now that we have completed Lent and Holy Week, let us renew the baptismal promises we made to serve God faithfully in his weak but blessed church.

Do you reject Satan?

Chorus: I do.

Leader: And all his works?

Chorus: I do.

Leader: Do you reject sin, so as to live in the freedom of God's children?

Chorus: I do.

Leader: Do you reject the glamor of evil and promise to work hard not to be mastered by sin?

Chorus: I do.

Leader: Do you believe in God, the creator of all things?

Chorus: I do.

Leader: Do you believe in Jesus, born of the Virgin Mary, who suffered under Pontius Pilate and was raised from the dead by the Father?

Chorus: I do.

Leader: Do you believe in the Holy Spirit, God's Pilgrim Church, the Communion of Saints, the forgiveness of sins, the resurrection of the body, and life everlasting?

Chorus: I do.

Leader: God, ever-living and ever-loving, through Jesus you have given us a new birth by water and the Holy Spirit, and have forgiven all our sins. Though we are weak and sometimes fall, keep us faithful to our Lord Jesus, whose love never falters.

Chorus: Amen.

Then follows the usual Communion Service: The Our Father, Lamb of God, Lord, I am not worthy, Communion, and closing prayer and blessing.

CLOSING HYMN

The strife is o'er, the battle done.
The victory of life is won.
The song of triumph has begun:
Alleluia!

The powers of death have done their worst,
but Christ their legions has dispersed.
Let shouts of holy joy outburst:
Alleluia!

PEACE TO YOU

PENTECOST

If there is Mass, the priest will wear the traditional red vestments, a sign of the tongues of fire of Pentecost. Participants might be encouraged to wear some red clothing, and perhaps red balloons or red carnations might be in evidence.

OPENING HYMN *(sung or played)*

Come, Holy One, Creator blest,
and in our hearts take up thy rest;
come with thy grace and heav'nly aid
to fill the hearts which thou hast made.

O Comforter, to thee we cry,
thou gift of God, sent from on high,
thou font of life and fire of love,
the soul's anointing from above.

Leader: Let us begin our worship together in the name of the Father and of the Son and of the Holy Spirit.

Chorus: Amen.

Leader: The grace of our Lord Jesus Christ and the love of God and the communion of the Holy Spirit be with you all.

Chorus: And also with you.

Leader: My brothers and sisters, to prepare ourselves to take part in this sacred liturgy, let us first call to mind our sins:

Chorus: I confess to Almighty God,
and to you, my brothers and sisters,
that I have greatly sinned,
in my thoughts and in my words,
in what I have done and in what I have failed
to do,
through my fault, through my fault, through
my most grievous fault.
Therefore I ask Blessed Mary ever-virgin,
all the angels and saints,
and you my brothers and sisters
to pray for me to the Lord our God.

Leader: May Almighty God have mercy on us, forgive us our sins, and bring us to life everlasting. Amen.

Chorus: Glory to God in the highest,
and peace to his people on earth.
Lord God, heavenly King,
Almighty God and Father.
We worship you, we give you thanks,
we praise you for your glory.
Lord Jesus Christ, only Son of the Father,
Lord God, Lamb of God,
you take away the sin of the world,
have mercy on us.
You are seated at the right hand of the Father,
receive our prayer.
For you alone are the Holy One,
you alone are the Lord,
you alone are the Most High,
Jesus Christ, with the Holy Spirit,
in the glory of God the Father. Amen.

Leader: Let us pray (*short pause here*):
O Lord of light, from whom every good gift comes, send your Spirit into our lives with the power of a mighty wind and by the flame of your wisdom open the windows of our minds. Loosen our tongues to sing your praise in words beyond the power of speech, for without your Spirit we could never raise our voices to speak what is right or announce the truth that Jesus is Lord, the one who lives and reigns with you and the Holy Spirit, one God, for ever and ever.

Chorus: Amen.

Leader: A reading from the Acts of the Apostles (2:1–11):
The day of Pentecost found the disciples gathered in one place. Suddenly, from the sky there came a noise like a strong, driving wind that shook the house they were in. Tongues, as of fire, appeared. These tongues parted and came to rest on each of them and all were filled with the Holy Spirit. Amazingly,

they found they could express themselves in foreign tongues and make bold proclamations as the Spirit prompted them.

Now, staying in Jerusalem at the time were visitors, devout Jews of every nation under heaven. These too heard the sound and gathered together in a large crowd, confused because each one heard the disciples speaking in his own language. Completely astonished, they asked, "Are not all of those who are speaking Galileans? Then how come each of us is hearing them in our native tongue? After all, among us there are Parthians and Medes and Elamites, folk from Mesopotamia, Judea, Cappadocia, Pontus, Phrygia, Pamphylia, Egypt, and parts of Libya. Why, there are even visitors from Rome, both Jews and converts to Judaism. There are Cretan and Arabs too, yet each of us hears them speaking in our own native tongue about the marvels that God has accomplished."

The Word of the Lord.

Chorus: Thanks be to God.

RESPONSORIAL PSALM
(Psalm 104: 1, 24, 29–31, 34)

Leader: Lord, send out your Spirit and renew the face of the earth.

Chorus: Lord, send out your Spirit and renew the face of the earth.

Leader: Bless the Lord, O my soul!
　　　　O Lord, you are great indeed!
　　　　How varied are your works, O Lord.
　　　　The earth is full of your creatures.

Chorus: Lord, send out your Spirit and renew the face of the earth.

Leader: If you take away their breath, they perish
　　　　and return to their dust.
　　　　When you send forth your spirit, they are created
　　　　and you renew the face of the earth.

Chorus: Lord, send out your Spirit and renew the face of the earth.

Leader: May the glory of the Lord endure forever.
May the Lord be glad in his works.
Pleasing to him be my song;
I will be glad in the Lord.

Chorus: Lord, send out your Spirit and renew the face of the earth.

THE SEQUENCE

Leader: Come, Holy Spirit, come!
And from your celestial home
shed a ray of light divine.

Chorus: Come, Father of the poor,
come, source of all our store,
come, within our bosoms shine.

Leader: O most blessed Light divine,
shine within these hearts of thine,
and our inmost being fill.

Chorus: Heal our wounds, our strength renew,
on our dryness pour your dew.
Wash the stains of guilt away.

Leader: Bend the stubborn heart and will,
melt the frozen, warm the chill.
Guide the steps that go astray.

Chorus: Give us virtue's sure reward.
Give us your salvation, Lord.
Give us joys that never end. Amen.

Leader: A reading of the Holy Gospel according to John (20:19–23):
On the evening of the first day of the week, even though the disciples had locked the door to the place where they were hiding for fear of the authorities, Jesus suddenly came and stood before them. He said, "Shalom, peace be with you." While they were still frozen in amazement, he showed them his wounded hands and side. The disciples went from shock to joy. Once

more, Jesus said, reassuringly, "Shalom." Then he paused and said, "As the Father has sent me, so I am sending you." Then, quite deliberately, he breathed on them and said, "Receive the Holy Spirit. If you forgive people's sins, they are forgiven them. If you hold them bound, they are held bound."

The gospel of the Lord.

Chorus: Praise to you, Lord Jesus Christ.

Reflection or homily. If the Leader feels confident in managing this process, they might want to invite reflections from participants on the Seven Gifts of the Holy Spirit: Wisdom, Fortitude, Knowledge, Understanding, Counsel, Piety, and Fear of the Lord. Better still, you might want to retrieve the engaging Pentecost homily in Appendix 1 ("The Holy Spirit and Papa God"), read it carefully, and invite people to share a story of when a "tree grew where it shouldn't"—that is, where the unexpected grace of the Holy Spirit surprisingly appeared. The Leader must be strongly directive here: Set a time limit of 3–4 minutes and a limited number of people (but more than one; no one-man or one-woman show). No "this is my life" marathons. Each person would come to the microphone and share a story. Since bishops tend to get nervous about lay people "preaching," you can call it a witness talk.

THE APOSTLES' CREED

Chorus: I believe in God
      the Father Almighty,
      Creator of heaven and earth,
      and in Jesus Christ, his only Son, our Lord,
      who was conceived by the Holy Spirit,
      born of the Virgin Mary,
      suffered under Pontius Pilate,
      was crucified, died and was buried.
      He descended into hell.
      On the third day he rose again from the dead;
      he ascended into heaven
      and is seated at the right hand of God the
            Father Almighty.
      From there he will come to judge the living
            and the dead.

I believe in the Holy Spirit,
the Holy Catholic Church,
the communion of saints,
the forgiveness of sins,
the resurrection of the body,
and life everlasting. Amen.

PRAYERS OF THE FAITHFUL *(Feel free to create your own)*

Proceed with the usual ending of a liturgy, everyone holding red balloons, with a bit of Beethoven tossed in:

Joyful, joyful we adore thee
God of glory, Lord of love;
hearts unfold like flowers before thee
op'ning to the sun above.

All thy works with joy surround thee,
earth and heav'n reflect thy rays.
Stars and angels sing around thee,
center of unbroken praise.

Melt the clouds of sin and sadness,
drive the dark of doubt away.
Giver of immoral gladness,
fill us with the light of day.

Field and forest, vale and mountain,
flow'ry meadow, flashing sea,
chanting bird and flowing fountain
call us to rejoice in thee.

DEVOTIONS
{ *and* **REMEMBRANCES**

ALL SOULS' DAY

Anote: Subscribe to your diocesan newspaper. In November, most of them publish a list of all the religious and clergy who have died during the year, plus a letter from the bishop and some inspiring articles on death and hope. It's a way of keeping alert to the wider church, of connecting with others, of seeing yourself in the faith context of the People of God.

This service is brief and open to any ritual of imagination. Some have the names of deceased loved ones written down on scraps of paper that are collected and placed in a suitable box to be carried later to the nearby parish to rest in the sanctuary for a while. Others bury the box on the grounds with a short prayer or blessing. Some call out the names of one or two persons they want remembered. What follows is one suggestion for a simple gathering with a follow-up image of Mary, the sorrowful mother.

Leader: "Eternal rest grant to them, O Lord," is our wish for our deceased beloveds. We turn to the comfort of the scriptures, beginning with a reading from the Book of Daniel (10:1–2, 12:1–3):

I, Daniel, mourned, and I heard this word of the Lord:

"At that time, there shall arise Michael, the great prince, guardian of your people. It shall be a time unsurpassed in distress since nations began. At that time, your people shall escape—everyone who is found to be written in the book. Many of those who sleep in the dust of the earth shall awake. Some shall live forever. Others shall be an everlasting horror and disgrace. But the wise shall shine brightly, like the splendor of the firmament, and those who lead the many to justice shall be like the stars forever."

The word of the Lord.

Chorus: Thanks be to God.

Leader: A reading from the Holy Gospel according to John (14:1):

"Do not let your hearts be troubled. Believe in God; believe also in me. In my Father's house there are many dwelling places. If it were not so, would I have told you that I go to prepare a place for you? And if I go and prepare a place for you, I will come and will take you to myself so that where I am you may be also."

The gospel of the Lord.

Chorus: Praise to you, Lord Jesus Christ.

A REFLECTION

Leader: The one thing that all of us here have in common is loss. We might have lost our parents, our siblings, our spouses, our children—that memory is still painful—our grandchildren, our friends. [Here at a senior residence, we routinely see a notice posted of someone's death, perhaps people we got to know well.] People "of a certain age," especially those of us with serious illness, live with the spectrum of death daily, though we suppress thinking about it or engage in gallows humor to take the sting away.

But today, All Souls' Day, the Church challenges us to do precisely that: to think about death, not morbidly, but communally; not stoically, but hopefully. The Feast of All Souls, following yesterday's Feast of All Saints, invites us to recall that we are a part of the Communion of Saints, that we are in deep, mystic connection with those present, those past, those yet to come. We belong. We influence. We interact. We are children of the promise for, as we heard in the gospel, Jesus has prepared a place for us. Remember that gospel. Remember his words. Embrace them. Cherish them. To help you to do so, let me restate the gospel with a story, an image.

A long time ago, there lived a little boy whose parents had died. He was taken in by an aunt, who raised him as her own child. Years later, after he had grown up and left his aunt, he received a letter from her. She was in terminal illness and, from the tone of her letter, he knew she was afraid of death. This man, whom she had raised and touched, wrote her a letter in which he said:

It is now thirty-five years since I, a little boy of six, was left quite alone in the world. You sent me word that you would give me a home and be a mother to me. I've never forgotten the day when I made the long journey of ten miles to your house. I can still recall my disappointment when, instead of coming for me yourself, you sent your servant, Caesar, a dark man, to fetch me. I well remember my tears and my anxiety as, perched high on your horse and clinging tight to Caesar, I rode off to my new home.

Night fell before we finished the journey and, as it grew dark, I became even more afraid. "Do you think she'll go to bed before I get there?" I asked Caesar anxiously. "Oh, no," said Caesar, "she'll surely stay up for you. When we get out of these woods, you'll see her light shining in the window."

Presently, we did ride out into the clearing and there was your light. I remember that you were waiting at the door; that you put your arms tight around me; that you lifted me—a tired, frightened little boy—down from the horse. You had a fire burning on the hearth, a hot supper waiting on the stove. After supper, you took me to my new room. You heard me say my prayers. Then you sat with me until I fell asleep.

You probably realize why I am trying to recall this to your memory now. Very soon, God is going to send for you, and take you to a new home. I'm trying to tell you that you needn't be afraid of the summons, or of the strange journey, or of the dark messenger of death. God can be trusted. God can be trusted to do as much for you as you did for me so many years ago. At the end of the road, you'll find love and a welcome waiting. And you'll be safe in God's care. I'm going to watch and pray for you until you're out of sight. And I

shall wait for the day when I make the same journey myself and find you waiting at the end of the
road to greet me.

A lovely story for All Souls. Notice the metaphors and sym-
bols: Caesar, the dark figure, is death; the light at the end of the
journey is Jesus, the light of the world. The house is the "many
rooms" in the Father's house that Jesus promised. The supper is
the heavenly banquet. God is the loving aunt. It's a homecoming
story. It is gospel. It is promise. It takes the sting off our loss.[1]

So, joy and peace are the lot of those who went before us
and the hope that sustains us. The Feasts of All Saints and All
Souls remind us that we are joined, interconnected, united by
that One who has gone to prepare a place for them—and for us.

May our loved ones rest in peace. May we live in hope.

Finally, let's end with a few verses from an old favorite for
older Catholics, the haunting *Stabat Mater*:

Leader: At the cross her station keeping,
stood the mournful Mother weeping,
close to Jesus to the last.

Chorus: Through her heart his sorrow sharing,
all his bitter anguish bearing,
now at length the sword has passed.

Leader: Oh, how sad and sore distressed
was that Mother highly blessed
of the sole begotten One.

Chorus: Is there one who would not weep
'whelmed in miseries so deep,
Christ's dear Mother to behold?

Leader: O sweet Mother, font of love,
touch my spirit from above,
make my heart with yours accord.

. . . .

1   A version of this reflection was previously published in William J. Bausch, *Once
Upon a Gospel: Inspiring Homilies and Insightful Reflections* (New London, CT:
Twenty-Third Publications, 2008), 107–108.

Chorus: Make me feel as you have felt;
        make my soul to glow and melt
        with the love of Christ my Lord.

Leader: Christ, when you shall call me hence,
        be your mother my defense,
        be your cross my victory.

(a moment of silence)

Leader: Let us pray.
        God our Father,
        your power brings us to birth,
        your providence guides our lives
        and by your command we return to dust.
        Lord, we know that those who have died still
           live in your presence.
        Their lives change, but do not end.
        Still, we miss them beyond measure.
        We cherish their memories and, with those
           memories in our hearts,
        we move into the future, sustained by your
           grace and
        open to whatever challenge, service, and
           compassion
        we can do in their name.

        In company with Christ,
        who died and now lives
        —though we are heavy with loss and sadness,
        nevertheless, we rejoice in your
        Kingdom, where all our tears are wiped away.

        Unite us together one day as one family
        to sing your praise forever and ever.

Chorus: Amen.

"The effect of her being on those around her was incalculably diffusive: for the growing good of the world is partly dependent on unhistoric acts; and that things are not so ill with you and me as they might have been, is half owing to the number who lived faithfully a hidden life, and rest in unvisited tombs."

—George Eliot, *Middlemarch*

MAY CROWNING

I n the presence of a statue of Mary set up in a conspicuous place, this simple devotion can be celebrated at church or home or institution. The devotional elements are Marian hymns, the crowning, a reflection, the litany of Mary, the rosary, and a closing Marian hymn. Other options include pieces of paper on which are written prior supplications to the Virgin. After the crowning, these are burned in a cylinder (if the devotion takes place outside). Inside, the petitions can be placed in a decorated box, which can later be brought to the local Catholic Church to rest beneath the statue of Mary.

OPENING HYMN—*the traditional hymn for the crowning:*

Immaculate Mary, your praises we sing.
You reign in splendor with Jesus our king.
Ave, Ave, Ave, Ave Maria.
Ave, Ave Maria.

The crowning takes place to the traditional tune of

"O Mary we crown thee with blossoms today
Queen of the angels, Queen of the May..."

followed by placing the petitions in a container or, for seniors, the leader may go around the room with the container and collect petitions.

REFLECTION

LITANY

Leader: Let us join in the litany of Mary:

Lord, have mercy on us.	*Christ, have mercy on us.*
Lord, have mercy on us.	*Christ, hear us.*
God the Father of heaven,	*have mercy on us.*
God the Son, redeemer of the world,	*have mercy on us.*
God the Holy Spirit,	*have mercy on us.*
Holy Trinity, one God,	*have mercy on us.*
Holy Mary,	*pray for us.*
Holy Mother of God,	*pray for us.*
Holy virgin of virgins,	*pray for us.*
Mother of Christ,	*pray for us.*
Mother of the Church,	*pray for us.*
Mother of Divine Grace,	*pray for us.*
Mother most pure,	*pray for us.*
Mother most chaste,	*pray for us.*
Mother inviolate,	*pray for us.*
Mother most admirable,	*pray for us.*
Mother of Good Counsel,	*pray for us.*
Mother of our Creator,	*pray for us.*
Mother of our Savior,	*pray for us.*
Mother of mercy,	*pray for us.*
Virgin most prudent,	*pray for us.*
Virgin most venerable,	*pray for us.*
Virgin most renown,	*pray for us.*
Virgin most powerful,	*pray for us.*
Virgin most faithful,	*pray for us.*

Mirror of justice,	*pray for us.*
Seat of wisdom,	*pray for us.*
Cause of our joy,	*pray for us.*
Vessel of honor,	*pray for us.*
Mystical Rose,	*pray for us.*
Tower of David,	*pray for us.*
Tower of Ivory,	*pray for us.*
Gate of heaven,	*pray for us.*
Morning star,	*pray for us.*
Refuge of sinners,	*pray for us.*
Comforter of the afflicted,	*pray for us.*
Queen of angels,	*pray for us.*
Queen of Apostles,	*pray for us.*
Queen of all saints,	*pray for us.*
Queen of peace,	*pray for us.*
Lamb of God, who takes away the sins of the world,	*spare us, O Lord.*
Lamb of God, who takes away the sins of the world,	*graciously hear us, O Lord.*
Lamb of God, who takes away the sins of the world,	*have mercy on us, O Lord.*

Leader: Pray for us, O Holy Mother of God,

Chorus: That we may be made worthy of the promises of Christ.

Leader: Let us pray. Grant, we beseech you, O Lord God, that we your servants may enjoy perpetual health of mind and body and, by the glorious intercession of the Blessed Virgin Mary, be delivered from present sorrow and enjoy everlasting happiness. Through Christ our Lord,

Chorus: Amen.

CLOSING MARIAN HYMN

An option: In an unusual step, I have inserted this following revelatory homily about Mary because it is so fundamentally basic and, every now and then, needs to be told. You may want to incorporate it into the May Crowning liturgy somehow, or perhaps share it as an antecedent in reciting the rosary together. Be creative. This homily is a corrective we all need.

A HOMILY ON MARY

The woman named Mary whom we honor today, and about whom we know so little, has intrigued us for twenty centuries. We don't know when she was born or when she died, but we can place her in history. We know where she lived and tradition names some of her friends and family. But why does she persist through the ages? What is her appeal? The answer is to be found in her human journey with God—which is, in reality, our journey.

When we first meet her, Mary is the object of an ugly rumor: She is pregnant without yet having a husband. Her fiancé, Joseph, decides officially to deny her, reject anything about the pregnancy, and put her at a distance. That she was innocent, invaded by the Spirit, he could not believe. So, right away, we understand why people down through the ages who have suffered from false rumors, who have had their reputations soiled, who have been misunderstood and maligned, and unwed mothers, have all identified with her.

Then, too, there was her very human anxiety and fear. "What's this all about anyway—this Mother of God business?" she wondered. "How can this be?" she asked the angel incredulously. "What does God want? What about Joseph? How can this happen? How can I do this?"

Confused, scared, and full of questions, Mary is all those people, throughout the ages, who have cried out, "How can I tackle this challenge? How can I survive? What does God want of me? What's it all about?"

When her son was born, shepherds and angels rejoiced, but power brokers seethed and conspired to kill her baby. They wanted his life, his spirit. Parents today and down through the ages, faced with so many soul assassins, have immediately identified with Mary. They know well enough that there are people out there waiting to kill their children. There are people who are waiting to sell their children drugs; the media, which glamorizes uncommitted sex; the hawkers, with cash registers for hearts, who teach them that we *do* live by bread alone; the soul snatchers of false values—all are after their children to kill their spirits. Parents know what Mary knew and fear what she feared.

Mary had to flee with her husband and child and become a refugee in a foreign land. She immediately joins the countless displaced persons—the homeless huddling in the world's doorways and sleeping on the nation's grates, and the 27 million refugees walking the earth today—these lowly who need to be lifted up. They are cousins under the skin, and they can identify with Mary.

Mary loses her child when he is an adolescent. She becomes every parent, every teacher, every mentor in history who can't communicate with a teenager; who loses them to gangs or drugs; whose kids have joined the small army of runaways roaming the streets, exploited by the sex trade, abused and beaten. Many can identify with Mary here.

At some point—we don't know when—this wife and mother became a widow. She buried her husband. Everyone who has lost a spouse, cried Mary's tears, felt the gnawing void in their belly, and returned to an empty bed can identify with her.

When her son is old enough, he leaves home to begin his mission. He leaves a widowed mother behind and suddenly every mother and father who sees their children grow up and leave them behind—especially those left behind in nursing homes—knows what she is feeling in her heart.

When Mary walks the streets, now that she is alone, she has to give way to the rough Roman soldiers and leering men passing by. She has to move quickly and live in the shadows. As a minority woman in an occupied territory, as a widow with no man around, she is always subject to sexual and physical exploitation and discrimination. Everyone with no rights, every minority figure who has had to swallow their pride, everyone ever called nigger or wop or fag, can identify with Mary.

When she hears rumors that her son is preaching nearby, she goes with some relatives to see him, but can't get near him because of the crowds. She has to be content with sending word that she's out there on the fringe. The message arrives to Jesus that his mother and relatives want to see him and he, gesturing to the crowd, asks, "Who are my mother and brothers and sisters? Everyone who does the will of God is my mother and brother and sister." It sounded like a put-down, a message to tell his mother to go home, but she read it for what it said, what she always knew: Her glory was not primarily that she was his biological mother, but that she was closer to him than anyone else because she loved God and, even when she didn't understand it, did his will. And every little person on the sideline, off-center, on the fringe, who doesn't understand what's going on, but simply clings fast to God's will, can identify with Mary.

And then that son is caught—betrayed by one who had come over for dinner many a time, brought to a mock trial, beaten, humiliated, and hung on a public cross. She arrives in time to see him hanging there, every inch of her mind and body straining to go to him, but she is forced by the soldiers to keep her distance. And suddenly, every parent who has seen their child on a cross—every parent who has seen their child carted off to prison, every parent who wants more than anything else in the world to help their grown children dealing with alcoholism, living in sin, raising their children on nothing, not even having them baptized, going through a divorce—every parent who witnesses such "crucifixions," but who must keep their distance, who are *told* to keep their distance, can identify with Mary and must pray and suffer in silence.

Finally, Mary cradles the broken, dead body of her only son in her arms and sobs uncontrollably, and there she is once more: every parent who has lost a child, any friend who has lost a friend, any classmate who has lost a classmate, through overdose or gunshot, accident or disease, can identify with Mary of the Pieta.

This is the woman—this pilgrim who savored the ups and downs of life—*this* is the ageless woman who has been given to us as a legacy. "Son, behold thy mother." And here we are today, beholding her. But it's good to remember that we're beholding her now that it's all over. The Church has, frankly, romanticized her. It clothes her with the sun, puts the moon beneath her feet, haloes her head with stars, dresses her in medieval robes, paints in winged cherubs to do her bidding, places her against a background of Italian villas, and has her whisked up into heaven to the sound of Handel's *Messiah*.

But we should understand that that's all metaphor, figures of speech, storytelling. What it means to say—all this heavenly glamor—is that Mary, who is Everywoman, and Everyman, is blessed now because, though unblessed in many ways in life, she remained faithful. In all the unfairness of life, she clung to God. In virginity, in motherhood, in widowhood, at home, as a wanderer in a foreign land, with a live child, with a dead child, she clung to God. So, she becomes a woman for all ages, and that is the secret of her enduring popularity and her appeal.

And the Church elevates her, not because she started out as great and traveled a privileged path, but because she was a handmaid of the Lord and traveled the lowly path. But then, he who is mighty has done great things for her. He has lifted her up when she was down, fed her when she was hungry, and because she responded to his loving invitation wherever life would lead her, saw to it that all generations would call her blessed.

That's what we're doing right now: calling this woman of our flesh and blood, our experience, blessed. Which is not honoring someone far away and high above us. No, we're calling blessed someone near, who is right with us at every human step. And the celebration of God's taking her into heaven is a sign of hope for us. It is meant to be a preview of coming attractions for all who cling to God in perplexity and adversity. Mary, the Church says in the Assumption, is what we shall be. She is promise fulfilled, humanity completed, faithfulness rewarded. Simply put, she is us at the end of the journey we are travelling. That is why Mary is so compelling. She is indeed a Woman for All Times and All Seasons.[1]

1   A version of this homily was previously published in Bausch, *An Anthology of Saints*, 28-32.

SACRAMENT OF THE SICK

This is an official liturgy that requires a priest, although it is my guess that, in due time, because of the shortage, we will see deacons take up the task.

Because, for centuries, only people about to die were anointed, the Church used the sacramental title of Extreme Unction to emphasize its near-death use. When you saw the priest coming with his oils, you knew the end was near. Finally, belatedly recognizing that the sacrament is an extension of Jesus' healing ministry, the Church changed the name to Sacrament of the Sick to emphasize precisely that. Anyone who is physically or mentally ill may receive the sacramental touch of Christ.

Mostly, in practice, the Sacrament of the Sick is administered one-on-one, as the need arises, but it is best celebrated, as the term *liturgy* implies, communally. As a pastor, I would issue a notice for anyone who wished to be anointed to sign up (to control the numbers) for a Mass of anointing. At St. Mary's, we invited the town's caregivers, like the emergency squad (Roman Catholic or not) to attend and receive the community's gratitude and blessing.

The following communal anointing does not include the Mass and is envisaged as being celebrated in a nursing home or senior residence. Although not a liturgy, I have included it so that participants may take an active part in the ritual when the occasion arises, such as reading the scripture and the responses.

Lector: A reading from Romans (8:14–17):

Everyone moved by the Spirit is a child of God. The spirit you received is not the spirit of slaves, bringing fear into your lives again. Rather, it is the spirit of sons and daughters and it makes us cry out, "Abba!" The Spirit himself and our spirit bear united witness that we are children of God and, if we are children, heirs as well—heirs of God and co-heirs with Christ, sharing his suffering so as to share his glory.

The word of the Lord.

Chorus: Thanks be to God.

RESPONSORIAL PSALM *(Psalm 27)*

Lector: Put your hope in the Lord; take courage and be strong.

Chorus: Put your hope in the Lord; take courage and be strong.

Lector: The Lord is my light and my salvation.
Whom need I fear?
The Lord is the fortress of my life,
of whom shall I be afraid?

Chorus: Put your hope in the Lord; take courage and be strong.

Leader: One thing I ask of the Lord, one thing I seek:
to live in the house of the Lord all the days of
my life,
to enjoy the sweetness of the Lord and to
consult him in his temple.

Chorus: Put your hope in the Lord; take courage and be strong.

Lector: For he shelters me under his awning in times
of trouble.
He hides me deep in his tent, sets me on a
high rock.

Chorus: Put your hope in the Lord; take courage and be strong.

Lector: Lord, hear my voice as I cry! Pity me!
Answer me!
My heart has said of you, "Seek his face."
Lord, I do seek your face; do not hide your
face from me.

Chorus: Put your hope in the Lord; take courage and be strong.

Lector: Do not repulse your servant in anger;
you are my help.
Never leave me, never desert me, God,
my Savior!
If my father and mother will desert me, the
Lord will care for me still.

Chorus: Put your hope in the Lord; take courage and be strong.

Lector: A reading from the Epistle of I Peter (1:3–9):

Blessed be God, the Father of our Lord Jesus Christ, who, in his great mercy, has given us a new birth as his sons and daughters by raising Jesus from the dead so that we have a sure hope and the promise of an inheritance that cannot be spoiled or soiled, and never fades away. . . . Through your faith, God's power will guard you. . . . This is a great joy for you, even though you may for a short time have to bear being plagued by all sorts of trials; so that when Jesus Christ is revealed, your faith will have been tested and proven like gold. Then you will have praise and glory and honor.

The word of the Lord.

Chorus: Thanks be to God.

Lector: Blest be God, the Father of our Lord Jesus Christ, for he has blessed us with every spiritual gift in Christ.

A reading of the Holy Gospel according to John (4:46–54):

After Jesus left Samaritan territory and returned to Galilee, a royal official whose son was ill sought him out and begged him to heal his son, for the boy was near death. Jesus remarked, "It's always the same: Unless you people see signs and wonders, you will not believe." But the official ignored the remark and pleaded, "Sir, please. Please come down before my little boy dies." Jesus, moved by the man's grief, replied, "Go home. Your son will live." The man believed Jesus and started back home. As he was on his way, his servants met him and told him that his son was well, was alive. The official asked them when this recovery had happened and they replied, "Yesterday, in the afternoon, the fever suddenly left him." The official then realized that it was the very same hour that Jesus had told him his son would live. So, he and his whole household became believers.

The Gospel of the Lord.

Chorus: Praise to you, Lord Jesus Christ.

HOMILY

PRAYERS

Celebrant: Let us pray now to the Lord for our sick brothers and sisters, and for all those dedicated to serving and caring for them:

That God would look kindly on our sick brothers and sisters, let us pray to the Lord.

Chorus: Lord, hear our prayer.

Celebrant: That the Spirit would give strength to their bodies and minds, let us pray to the Lord.

Chorus: Lord, hear our prayer.

Celebrant: That God would ease our brothers' and sisters' sufferings, let us pray to the Lord.

Chorus: Lord, hear our prayer.

Celebrant: That God would free them from temptation and sin, let us pray to the Lord.

Chorus: Lord, hear our prayer.

Celebrant: That the Lord God would sustain all the sick with his strong power, let us pray to the Lord.

Chorus: Lord, hear our prayer.

Celebrant: That God would give life and health to our brothers and sisters, on whom we are about to lay our hands in his name, let us pray to the Lord.

Chorus: Lord, hear our prayer.

The Blessing of the Oil *(if not already blessed)*

Celebrant: Lord God, loving Father, you bring healing to the sick through your son Jesus Christ. Hear us as we pray to you in faith and send the Holy Spirit, our helper and friend, upon this oil, whose nature has provided to serve the needs of all.

May your blessing come upon all who are anointed with this oil, that they may be freed from pain and illness and made well again in body, mind, and soul. Father, may this oil be blessed for our use in the name of our Lord Jesus Christ, who lives and reigns with you, forever and ever.

Chorus: Amen.

The anointing takes place, first on the forehead:

Celebrant: Through this holy anointing, may the Lord in his love and mercy help you with the grace of the Holy Spirit.

Chorus: Amen.

Celebrant Now on the upheld hands: May the Lord who frees you from sin save you and raise you up.

Chorus: Amen.

When all have been anointed, the Celebrant closes the liturgy.

Celebrant: Lord Jesus Christ, you shared in our human nature to heal the sick and save all humankind. Mercifully listen to our prayers for the physical and spiritual health of our brothers and sisters whom we have anointed in your name. May your protection console them and your strength make them well again. Help them to find hope in your suffering, for you have given them a share in your passion, you who are Lord, forever and ever.

Chorus: Amen.

THE VIGIL OR WAKE SERVICE

Here are the Church's official words concerning the wake service:

> The Vigil Service usually takes place during the period of visitation and viewing at the funeral home. . . . The Vigil Service can take the form of a Service of the Word with readings from Sacred Scripture accompanied by reflection and prayers. It can also take the form of one of the prayers of the Office for the Dead from the *Liturgy of the Hours.* The clergy and your funeral director can assist in planning such a service.[1]

As you can see, the official line is to leave the particulars of the wake up to the local parish where, in most parishes today, an established lay committee takes over. So, here is but one example of a wake service without a priest.

⟊∞∞∞⟊

Leader: In the name of the Father and of the Son and of the Holy Spirit.

Chorus: Amen.

Leader: The grace and peace of the Lord Jesus Christ and the love of God and the fellowship of the Holy Spirit be with you all.

Chorus: And also with you.

Leader: Let us pray:

Father of Mercy, who dries the tears of those who mourn, look upon your servant *N* who has departed from this life. Give

---

1   "An Overview of Catholic Funeral Rites," *United States Conference of Catholic Bishops,* https://www.usccb.org/prayer-and-worship/sacraments-and-sacramentals/bereavement-and-funerals/overview-of-catholic-funeral-rites.

him/her the fullness of your embrace. Welcome *him/her* into a place prepared for them by Jesus, who overcame death and makes all things new again. Soothe our own hearts, burdened with sorrow. Fill our emptiness with memories and our loss with hope. We ask this through Christ our Lord.

Chorus: Amen.

Leader: A reading from St. Paul's epistle to the Romans (14:7–9):
Brothers and sisters, remember this truth: We do not live to ourselves and we do not die to ourselves. If we live, we live to the Lord and if we die, we die to the Lord. So, then, whether we live or whether we die, we are the Lord's.
The word of the Lord.

Chorus: Thanks be to God.

RESPONSORIAL PSALM *(Psalm 23)*

Leader: The Lord is my Shepherd.

Chorus: The Lord is my Shepherd.

Leader: The Lord is my shepherd;
there is nothing I shall want.
Fresh indeed are the pastures
where he offers me sweet repose.

Chorus: The Lord is my Shepherd.

Leader: Near placid waters he leads me
to revive my drooping spirit.
He guides me along the right path,
for he is true to his name.

Chorus: The Lord is my Shepherd.

Leader: If I should walk in the very valley of darkness,
no evil would I fear
because you are there with your staff
to give me comfort and protection.

Chorus: The Lord is my Shepherd.

Leader: You have prepared a banquet for me
        in the sight of my foes.
        My head you have anointed with oil;
        indeed, my cup is overflowing.

Chorus: The Lord is my Shepherd.

Leader: Surely goodness and kindness shall follow me
        all the days of my life.
        In the Lord's own house shall I dwell,
        for ever and ever.

Chorus: The Lord is my Shepherd.

Leader: A Reading of the Holy Gospel according to John (11:17–44):

When Jesus arrived at Bethany, he found that his friend Lazarus had already been in the tomb four days. . . . Martha, Lazarus' sister, said to Jesus, "Lord, if you had been here, my brother would not have died. Still, I know that God will give you whatever you ask of him." Jesus replied, "Martha your brother will rise again . . . for I am the resurrection and the life. Those who believe in me will never die. Do you believe what I am saying?" Martha replied, "Yes, Lord, I do. I believe that you are the Messiah, the Son of God." . . .

Mary, weeping, joined her sister. The whole crowd was weeping. Jesus inquired where they had put Lazarus. Weeping himself, Jesus arrived at the tomb with the crowd. It was a cave with a large stone across it. Jesus ordered them to take away the stone, in spite of Martha's concern about the stench. Jesus paused, looked up to heaven, and exclaimed, "Father, I thank you for having heard me. I knew you always hear me, but I said this because of the crowd here, so that they may believe that you sent me." Then, with a loud voice, Jesus commanded, "Lazarus, come out!" The dead man came out, his hands and feet bound with strips of cloth and likewise his face. Jesus said to the bystanders, "Untie him and set him free."

The gospel of the Lord.

Chorus: Praise to you, Lord Jesus Christ.

There may be a reflection here or, better, a eulogy if there is to be one. Note that this is the place for the eulogy, not at the Requiem Mass. In fact, as a pastor, I would never permit a eulogy at the Mass (and some bishops have issued that rule for their dioceses). Some eulogies are fine, but mostly they are too long. Some are entertainment, some vulgar, and others quite foreign to the spirit of the liturgy.

After the eulogy, some music may be played or sung. Then the following Intercessions may be added:

Leader: Our *brother (sister)* was brought into this faith community in baptism. May *he/she* now enjoy the communion of saints forever. Let us pray to the Lord.

Chorus: Lord, hear our prayer.

Leader: *N* shared with us the bread of life. May *he/she* be forever at the eternal banquet of the Lord. Let us pray to the Lord.

Chorus: Lord, hear our prayer.

Leader: That those of us gathered here out of kinship, friendship, and love may always remember and cherish the memories of *N*, who made a difference to so many, let us pray to the Lord.

Chorus: Lord, hear our prayer.

Leader: That we may honor the memory of *N* by a life well lived, let us pray to the Lord.

Chorus: Lord, hear our prayer.

Leader: Let us pray as our Lord taught us:

Chorus: Our Father. . . .

Leader: Gracious God, we entrust our *brother (sister)* to your mercy. Now that *he/she* is freed from all cares, give *him/her* happiness and peace forever. Welcome *him/her* into paradise, where there will be no more sickness or sorrow, no more weeping and pain, but only peace and joy. We ask this through Christ our Lord.

Chorus: Amen.

DISMISSAL BLESSING

Leader: May the Lord bless and keep you.
May the Lord let his face shine upon you
and be gracious to you.
May the Lord look upon you kindly
and grant you his peace.

Chorus: Amen.

Remember, the wake service is quite flexible and you may tailor it to your needs.

THANKSGIVING: FIVE KERNELS

This remembrance is to be read by someone at the Thanksgiving table.

Some families have a peculiar Thanksgiving custom. On Thanksgiving Day, they set on each dinner plate five kernels of dried corn. Then, going around the table, each family member relates five things for which they have been thankful that year. The custom derives from an old legend about the Pilgrims. They were undertaking a perilous journey from Plymouth, England to Virginia. In fact, so perilous was sea travel in those days that it was always suggested that one make out one's will before boarding ship!

The Pilgrims were blown off course, landing instead in New England. They suffered a harsh first winter. During the winter months, it was not unusual to have two or three deaths a day. By spring, nearly half their numbers had perished. It was said that, during the worst of it, each person had only five kernels of corn to eat each day—and they were grateful for that.

So, let's follow this tradition, take up our kernels, one at a time, and, in five offbeat, random, but related stories, contemplate what we might be thankful for.

First kernel: A new year aborning. Think of Disney's *The Lion King.* Think of the scene where the spirit of Mufasa appears in the sky and speaks to his prodigal son, Simba, who has been hiding out in the deepest, darkest jungle, reclining in a life of self-centeredness and greed where only he—number one—counts. He has quite forgotten that he was born to be king. The ghost of his father challenges his spiritual blindness. He says to his son, "You have become less than you are."

That's our first kernel. We look at it and say, "Thank you, God, for reminding us that you have come among us, have called us by name, have shared our humanity so that we may share your divinity. Yes, our dignity is that we *are* related. By taking our human condition on yourself, you have made us a royal priesthood, a holy nation, a people set apart. So, thank you for a new year about to be born, our second chance, that calls us back to who we are meant to be."

Second kernel: In one of his celebrated Lake Wobegon tales, that marvelous genius and storyteller, Garrison Keillor, speaks of his childhood Thanksgiving dinners, as the family gathered around the table and remembered the blessings of the past year. Uncle John usually gave the prayer, which caused everyone to squirm.

As Keillor said, "Everybody in the family knew that Uncle John couldn't pray without talking about how good God is and crying. . . . Sure enough, Uncle John prayed, talked about how good God is, and cried." Then Keillor adds these memorable words, "All of us knew that God loves us, but Uncle John has never gotten over it."

Third kernel: a horse. One of the most famous racehorses was Seabiscuit, as you may know from the movies and books about him. Seabiscuit was the son of a champion, but originally, he was not destined to be like his father. The reason is that he was chosen to be the goat, the shill, the second banana, the fool. This means he was forced to run with better horses so that they would gain confidence by beating him. So, when he raced, he did what he was trained to do: fail, lose. Because of this demeaning treatment, Seabiscuit eventually became an angry, almost uncontrollable horse that nobody really wanted.

But one day, a trainer, considered to be past his prime, and a jockey considered too big to ride, came along and were willing to take a chance with him. In taking on Seabiscuit, the trainer simply said, "You don't throw a life away just because it's been banged up a little." By and by, Seabiscuit began to thrive under the care of these people who believed in him.

Sometimes we have been treated poorly, made to feel we could never measure up, were a loser—perhaps others even called us that—but we know there is someone who has never,

ever thrown away a banged-up life, and so, in the incarnation, he embraced ours. For *that*, we thank you, Lord.

Fourth kernel: bell ringers. A man tells about an experience he had. "Just up the road from my home," he writes, "is a field with two horses in it. Now, from a distance, each horse looks like any other horse. But, if you stop your car, or are walking by, you will notice something quite amazing. Looking into the eyes of one horse, you will find that he is blind. Obviously, his owner has chosen not to have him put down, but to make a good home for him.

"Now, if you stand there long enough and listen a while, you will hear the sound of a bell. Looking around, you will see that it comes from the smaller horse in the field. Attached to the horse's halter is a small bell. The bell lets the blind friend know where the other horse is, so he can follow.

"If you continue to stand there long enough and watch these two friends, you'll see that the horse with the bell is always checking on the blind horse and that the blind horse will listen for the bell and then slowly walk to where the other horse is and nuzzle him, trusting that he will not be led astray. Later on, when the horse with the bell returns to the barn each evening, you will notice that it stops occasionally and looks back, making sure that the blind friend isn't too far behind and can still hear the bell. After checking, it then moves on, till they're both safely back in the barn."

And that story leads us to give thanks for all the bell ringers in our lives: parents who nurtured and supported us, good friends who stuck with us, teachers who believed in us—anyone who pulled us through, inspired us, and led us to a better, holier life. Thank you, friends of the past and present.

Fifth kernel: crosses. Toward the end of the movie *Little Big Man*, which starred Dustin Hoffman, there is a scene in which an Indian named Old Lodge Skins, sick and blind, knows he is dying and begins to pray to God a prayer of thanksgiving: "O Lord God, I thank you for having made me a human being. I thank you for having given me life and eyes to see and enjoy your world. But, most of all, I thank you for my sickness and my blindness, because I have learned more from these than from my health and from my sight."

Life has often been hurtful, painful, and mostly unfair, and many people have turned their backs on a God who seems to be indifferent, absent, and silent. We can sympathize with that. But it is also true that for many, hardship, betrayal, sickness, and loss have brought them to a new dimension, dragged them into a different, fuller life that they never imagined possible.

One thinks of John Bernardone, whose depression and imprisonment led him to become Francis of Assisi; or town drunk Matt Talbot, who became a model of piety and compassion; or parents whose children died of AIDS, setting up hospices and centers to minister to those who are sick; or simply those who have known trauma and loss but whose prayer life deepened and whose charity expanded—all those who, like Old Lodge Skins, learned more from their crosses than from their crowns.

So, yes, we thank you, Lord, for the crosses that shaped us, made us humble, and brought us to our knees—a good place to be.

So, there we are. On the brink of a new year, with Thanksgiving still fresh in our memories, we are giving a different kind of thanks today—in fact, five kernels' worth.

So, we pray:

> For reminding us who we are,
> for your loving us to the extremes of your life,
> for embracing our brokenness,
> for sending us bell ringers,
> for the crosses of concealed graces—
> for *all* these things, O Lord, we also
> give thanks.
>
> Amen.[1]

---

1   A version of this reflection was previously published in William J. Bausch, *The Story Revealed: Homilies that Sustain, Inspire, and Engage* (New London, CT: Twenty-Third Publications, 2013), 2–5.

LECTIO DIVINA

This is the only private devotion in this booklet. Along with saying the rosary, making a novena, and other devotions, it requires no community. I include it because, although less well-known, it is a rich source of spiritual growth. The Latin *lectio divina* simply means "divine reading," a term which means reading the Bible, especially the gospels, with tempo and imagination. Tempo means that you read a passage slowly, meditatively, like savoring dark chocolate. Take your time. Be attentive. Take as long (or short) a time as you want to. Imagination means getting into the story yourself, maybe as a participant or an observer—whatever makes it like a movie you're caught up into. Don't hesitate to pause, close your eyes, and visualize the scene.

Let me share one example, a scripture that's good for troubled, all-is-lost, despairing times like our own. Let's go back to when Our Lord Jesus had been cruelly killed on Calvary and his followers were devastated as they saw their world collapse, themselves persecuted, and their faith shaken. Let me share the familiar gospel (John 20:11–18) of a distraught woman and a stranger.

Again, read it slowly and, more to the point, use your imagination to place yourself in the story.

> Mary Magdalene was standing outside the tomb where the dead body of Jesus had been buried. She was despairing, hurting, weeping. Suddenly, she thought she heard something. She turned around and she saw Jesus standing there, but she did not know it was Jesus. The person said to her, "Why are you weeping? Whom are you looking for?" Supposing him to be the gardener, she said to him, "Sir, if you have carried him away, tell me where you have put him and I will take him away." There was a silence and then the man simply said to her one word: "Mary!"

She recognized the familiar voice, quickly turned to him, and said, "Rabbouni!" Jesus replied, "Do not hold on to me because I have not yet ascended to the Father. But go to my brothers and say to them, "I am ascending to my Father and your Father, to my God and your God."

This time, with tears of joy rather than despair, Mary Magdalene immediately went and announced the good news, the stupendous news, to the disciples: "I have seen the Lord!" And she told them what he had said to her.

Let's review this gospel slowly and prayerfully, and let me freeze five "still pictures" for our contemplation.

The first tableau is the first encounter, when the man Mary supposes is the gardener asks her, "Why are you weeping?"

"I'm weeping," Mary responds, "because they have hurt and killed my master, a man with the face of God. I'm weeping because I miss him, because I can't even find his body. I miss him because he was our hope and now we are without hope."

We respond: "I'm weeping because I have lost my husband. I'm weeping because I lost my daughter to drugs, or my wife to Alzheimer's—my sweet love who doesn't even know my name anymore. I weep because my health is waning, because of the depression that never lets up, because the world is mad with slaughter and washes up three-year-old refugees on the shore, because all that I cherished is mocked, because my world seems utterly devoid of kindness and generosity, and charity is cold."

Yes, with Magdalene, we have a lot to weep about today, but go back in your imagination and be with Mary Magdalene in that garden of death. Listen. Someone has just asked *you* why you are weeping. Yes, there is Someone who wants to know. Someone is interested. Someone is there to listen. He has asked you a question. Answer him. Pour out your heart to him.

Next, ponder how Mary thought Jesus was a gardener: a gardener. This is strange, intriguing. Remember where she is. She is in the place where they bury dead people. She is at a tomb, a graveyard, a place of death. What is a gardener—one whose task is to sow life, green shoots, and bright flowers—what's a gardener doing in a place of death? He's planting hope.

That is something you might pause to pray over. In your place of weeping, of loss, of empty soul tombs, there is a gardener. Dare you believe? Is there a life-giver, a defier of death, hovering nearby? Did the gospel writer intend to put death and garden, stench and sweetness, darkness and brightness together to give you hope? There's a planter of seeds here. There is a perfume of hope in the air. Try to sense it.

The gardener speaks but one word—one personal, one very precious word: "Mary!" Not "woman," notice, or "hey, you," or "Ma'am." No, the gardener calls her by name. Let that sink in. She is not just one among countless millions, not just a face in the crowd, not an anonymous statistic, but "I know mine and mine know me" (John 10:14). "I no longer call you servants, but friends" (John 15:15).

What a lift of joy we feel when someone knows us and calls us by name. It's a one-to-one relationship in that gospel, and in your life. Jesus, the life-giving gardener, calls you by name. He knows you. This is music to your ears. He cares. Pause and listen for your name. You are not alone. You are not forgotten.

Jesus' instructions to Mary, at first sight, are odd, or maybe even sarcastic. What does he say? "Go to my *brothers* and say to them. . . ." "'*Brothers?*' Stop right there!" you might think. "He's got to be kidding. Some 'brothers'! One, the leader, the 'rock'— nice irony—shamelessly denied even knowing him. Another betrayed him. James and John wanted to be at his left and right in his kingdom, yet when he did enter it, they were nowhere to be found. Jesus had to be content with two thieves at this right and left. The others fled, weren't even around when he needed them most. They slept during his agony and the Roman soldiers couldn't even locate one of them to help Jesus carry his cross. They had to commandeer a stranger."

Jesus had every right to say, "Go to those deadbeats, those weaklings, those fair-weather friends"—but he doesn't. Instead, he calls these sad specimens of humanity "brothers." Think of that. How sweet the sound. How compassionate the heart. How forgiving the soul. How comforting the message. It tells you that you are not beyond the pale. Whatever you have done, whatever you feel, however hopeless you feel, how hurt, how much in the dark, you are brother. You are sister. You are Beloved. You must savor this one.

Finally, Mary Magdalene is told to go to the foundational apostles and announce the good news, the gospel, to *them*. Mary thereby becomes an apostle to the apostles. She goes to these dejected has-beens and gives *them* the good news: He is risen! She has herself become a gardener, planting life where there was death and despair. She reminds us that this is also our role in these terrible times: to plant seeds of hope in dark places, and words of comfort in dead places. The note, the phone call, the visit, the feeding of the hungry and clothing of the refugee, the sharing of the burden, and making things grow—especially faith, that it may be rekindled, and hope, that people might look upward again and find love in the small ministrations of life. These are the seeds that will "make all things new again" (Revelation 21:5).

So, I have suggested five places where you can enter into this gospel. You need only choose one or two, or go wherever the Spirit leads you. These were suggestions, possibilities, for reading the Bible with both mind and heart, of letting the sacred scripture speak to you, lift your spirits, and encourage you to encourage others.

The BLESSING OF THE THROATS

The Blessing of the Throats on Saint Blaise's feast day is a devotional blip. If you don't go to morning Mass—and most don't; it's a workday—you might run in to church for the quick candle embrace with a formula and then run off again. It's a minor sacramental occasion but, for many old-timers, it's a part of the overall Catholic culture, a note in the rhythm of the liturgical year that makes someone a Catholic. We love our saints and assign them specific tasks, giving unconscious testimony to the doctrine of the Communion of Saints, whereby we interconnect with one another regardless of time and space. Today our attention is directed toward Saint Blaise (more on him below).

⁓∝∝∝∝∝⁓

Leader: In the name of the Father, and of the Son, and of the Holy Spirit.

Chorus: Amen.

Leader: The grace and peace of God the Father and the Lord Jesus Christ be with you.

Chorus: And also with you.

Leader: Before we begin, a note about Saint Blaise. He entered the list of saints this way. Blaise was a bishop who was martyred in the city of Sebastea, Armenia, in 316. Some four hundred years later, he got a full-blown legend attached to his name called the *Acts of St. Blaise.* According to the legend, Blaise was a good bishop, working hard to encourage the spiritual and physical health of his people. Persecution raged in Armenia, even into the back country where he lived as a hermit in solitude and prayer, making friends with the wild animals. One day, a group of hunters seeking wild animals for use in the amphitheater stumbled upon Blaise's cave, only to observe him kneeling in prayer, surrounded by wolves, lions, and bears. The legend has it that, as the hunters hauled Blaise off to prison, a mother came with her young son who had a fish bone lodged in his throat. At Blaise's command, the child was able to cough up the bone—and that's where we get the blessing of the throats.

So, with that background behind us, let us move to the blessing.

A reading of the Holy Gospel according to Matthew (8:14–17):

When Jesus entered Peter's house, he saw Peter's mother-in-law lying in bed with a fever; he touched her hand and the fever left her, and she got up and began to serve him. That evening, they brought to him many who were possessed by demons; and he cast out the spirits with a word and cured all who were sick. This was to fulfill what had been spoken through the prophet Isaiah, "He took our infirmities and bore our diseases."

The gospel of the Lord.

Chorus: Praise to you, Lord Jesus Christ.

RESPONSORIAL PSALM *(Psalm 34:1–14)*

Leader: Taste and see the goodness of the Lord.

Chorus: Taste and see the goodness of the Lord.

Leader: I will bless the Lord at all times;
        his praise shall be ever in my mouth.
        Let my soul glory in the Lord;
        the lowly will hear me and be glad.

Chorus: Taste and see the goodness of the Lord.

Leader: Glorify the Lord with me,
        let us together extol his name.
        I sought the Lord, and he answered me
        and delivered me from all my fears.

Chorus: Taste and see the goodness of the Lord.

Leader: Look to him that you may be radiant with joy,
        and your faces may not blush with shame.
        When the afflicted called out, the Lord heard,
        and from all his distress he saved them.

Chorus: Taste and see the goodness of the Lord.

Leader: The angel of the Lord encamps
        around those who fear him and delivers them.
        Taste and see how good the Lord is;
        happy the one who takes refuge in him.

Chorus: Taste and see the goodness of the Lord.

Leader: Fear the Lord, you his holy ones,
        for nothing is lacking to those who fear him.
        The great grow poor and hungry;
        but those who seek the Lord want for no
          good thing.

Chorus: Taste and see the goodness of the Lord.

Leader: Come, children, hear me;
        I will teach you the fear of the Lord.
        Which of you desires life,
        and takes delight in prosperous days?

Chorus: Taste and see the goodness of the Lord.

Leader: Keep your tongue from evil
        and your lips from speaking guile.
        Turn from evil and do good;
        seek peace, and follow after it.

Chorus: Taste and see the goodness of the Lord.

A reflection may be given here.

THE INTERCESSIONS

Leader: Let us now pray for those who are sick and suffering. For those who care for the sick, and for all who seek the blessings of good health, we pray to the Lord.

Chorus: Lord, hear our prayer.

Leader: For those who suffer from sickness and disease, that they may receive healing, we pray to the Lord.

Chorus: Lord, hear our prayer.

Leader: For the mentally ill and for their families, that they may receive comfort, we pray to the Lord.

Chorus: Lord, hear our prayer.

Leader: For those with physical disabilities, that the strength of Christ may invigorate them, we pray to the Lord.

Chorus: Lord, hear our prayer.

Leader: For doctors and nurses, and for all who care for the sick, we pray to the Lord.

Chorus: Lord, hear our prayer.

Leader: For those who seek the prayers of Saint Blaise today, that they may be protected from afflictions of the throat and other forms of illness, we pray to the Lord.

Chorus: Lord, hear our prayer.

Leader: Let us now pray the Our Father.

Chorus: Our Father. . . .

The Blessing of the Throats. This may be done individually or by a simple extension of the hands over the group as a whole. If individually, some background music may be played.

Leader: Through the intercession of Saint Blaise, bishop and martyr, may God deliver you from every disease of the throat and from every other ailment, in the name of the Father, and of the Son, + and of the Holy Spirit.

Each person responds: Amen.

Leader: Almighty God, we thank you for your saints, who gave us a glimpse of what you must be like: the Lord of compassion and kindness. Listen to our prayers and make us worthy disciples and witnesses to your love. We ask this through Christ our Lord.

Chorus: Amen.

Leader: Go in peace.

Chorus: Thanks be to God.

BENEDICTION OF THE
MOST BLESSED SACRAMENT

This is a very popular Roman Catholic devotion, often used as an ending to some other devotion. At other times, it may serve as the backdrop for all-day adoration, when the Blessed Sacrament is exposed in the morning and reposed with Benediction at the end of the day. In this latter case, the priest, after morning Mass, will insert the lunette (the round, watch-like container of the Host) into a splendid monstrance, incense it, and leave it on the altar all day. Parishioners will sign up for an hour in rotation to be present in church and return in the evening when the priest will repose the Host with the Benediction rite. Again, this is an old and cherished devotion, so much so that most people can sing the Latin hymns by memory, which is why I include them.

When a priest is not available, a layperson, officially commissioned by the pastor, may open the tabernacle door and leave it at that. Come closing time, the layperson simply closes the tabernacle door and conducts Benediction. Lay leaders may follow this script, the only exception being that they may not bless the congregants with the monstrance:

> In the absence of an ordinary minister, an instituted acolyte, an Extraordinary Minister of Holy Communion, or a member of a religious community or lay association dedicated to eucharistic adoration and who has received approval from the local Ordinary may open the tabernacle and, if appropriate, place the ciborium on the altar or the host in the monstrance. At the conclusion of the period of adoration, these persons should replace the Blessed Sacrament in the tabernacle without blessing those present with the Eucharist. . . .

No special vesture is required of Extraordinary Ministers of Holy Communion or others who are not ordinary ministers when exposing the Blessed Sacrament.[1]

RITE OF EUCHARISTIC EXPOSITION AND BENEDICTION EXPOSITION OF THE BLESSED SACRAMENT

When the Leader goes to the tabernacle and opens it, all kneel. The Leader puts the lunette in the monstrance and exposes it on the altar, then goes to the sanctuary and kneels on the altar steps. Meanwhile, the congregation begins to sing:

O saving Victim, open wide	*O Salutaris Hostia*
The gate of heaven to us below.	*Quae caeli pandis ostium.*
Our foes press on from every side;	*Bella premunt hostilia;*
Your aid supply, your strength bestow.	*Da robur, fer auxilium.*
To your great name be endless praise,	*Uni trinoque Domino*
Immortal Godhead, One in Three;	*Sit sempiterna gloria:*
O grant us endless length of days	*Qui vitam sine termino,*
In our true native land with thee. Amen.	*Nobis donet in patria. Amen.*

During this period, there may be appropriate prayers, songs, readings from scripture, and a brief homily to help the congregation focus its attention to the worship of the Lord. People may kneel or be seated for their private portion of adoration/devotion.

. . . .

1   Office of Liturgy, "Guidelines for the Worship of the Eucharist Outside of Mass" (Yonkers, NY: Archdiocese of New York, 2017), 6.

BENEDICTION

After a period of meditation and reflection, the Leader goes to the altar, genuflects, and kneels. All kneel and join in singing:

Down in adoration falling,	*Tantum ergo Sacramentum*
This great Sacrament we hail;	*Veneremur cernui:*
Over ancient forms of worship	*Et antiquum documentum*
Newer rites of grace prevail;	*Novo cedat ritui:*
Faith will tell us Christ is present,	*Praestet fides supplementum*
When our human senses fail.	*Sensuum defectui.*

To the everlasting Father,	*Genitori, Genitoque*
And the Son who made us free,	*Laus et iubilatio,*
And the Spirit, God proceeding	*Salus, honor, virtus quoque*
From them Each eternally:	*Sit et benedictio:*
Be salvation, honor, blessing,	*Procedenti ab utroque*
Might and endless majesty. Amen.	*Compar sit laudatio. Amen.*

All remain kneeling when the Leader stands and says or chants:

Leader: You have given them Bread from heaven. (*During Eastertide, add* Alleluia.)

Chorus: Having all sweetness within it. (*During Eastertide, add* Alleluia.)

Leader: Let us pray. O God, who in this wonderful Sacrament has left us a memorial of your Passion, grant us, we pray, so to revere the sacred mysteries of your Body and Blood that we may always experience in ourselves the fruits of your redemption, who live and reign with God the Father in the unity of the Holy Spirit, one God, for ever and ever.

Chorus: Amen.

Whereas a priest or deacon will use the monstrance to make the sign of the cross over the people, a layperson will omit this step. They will simply come back in front of the altar, kneel, and lead everyone in the Divine Praises.

Blessed be God.
Blessed be his holy name.
Blessed be Jesus Christ, true God and
    true man.
Blessed be the name of Jesus.
Blessed be his most Sacred Heart.
Blessed be his most Precious Blood.
Blessed be Jesus in the most holy sacrament
    of the altar.
Blessed be the Holy Spirit, the Paraclete.

Blessed be the great Mother of God, Mary
    most holy.
Blessed be her holy and Immaculate
    Conception.
Blessed be her glorious Assumption.
Blessed be the name of Mary, virgin
    and Mother.
Blessed be St. Joseph, her most chaste spouse.

Blessed be God in his angels and in his saints.
Amen.

The Leader then replaces the Blessed Sacrament in the tabernacle and genuflects. All stand and join in singing:

Holy God, we praise thy name; Lord of all, we
    bow before thee.
All on earth thy scepter claim; all in heaven
    above adore thee.
Infinite thy vast domain, everlasting is
    thy reign!
Hark, the loud celestial hymn angel choirs
    above are raising.

Cherubim and Seraphim, in unceasing chorus
  praising.
Fill the heavens with sweet accord: "Holy,
  holy, holy Lord!"

REMEMBERING 9/11

In case you're called upon to make some remarks at a memorial ceremony, here are some worthy words.

One of the more poignant photographs from the 9/11 Ground Zero tragedy is that of a firefighter, grimy and covered with soot, totally exhausted, kneeling against a fallen block with his head in his hands. He seems about to cry—and why not? Over 350 of his own firefighter buddies had been killed or were missing, along with 200 Port Authority employees, 40 police officers, 700 workers from each of the various financial companies in the twin towers, 266 people on the airplanes, nearly 200 at the Pentagon, and thousands more. There were many like him—police officers, emergency personnel, volunteers— all overwhelmed by the emotional and physical magnitude of the tragedy.

We were all emotionally and politically unprepared. For decades, we had seen in the movies and watched on television the horrors of war. We winced as whole villages were burned to the ground, the billowy smoke the only indication that men, women, and children once lived there. We looked aghast at the continuous black fumes from the Nazi gas chambers. We sat at a safe distance to watch the footage of the bombings of Britain, Poland, France, Germany, the Netherlands, and more. Cities, towns, hamlets, great castles, museums, cathedrals—all up in smoke. We watched with fascination the death-dealing mushroom clouds over Japan. In *Life* magazine, we checked out the photographs of the massive mounds of human skulls in the Cambodian killing fields.

And eventually, we all began to watch those horrors with a certain detachment, even those who lost loved ones in the wars, as Hollywood turned carnage into entertainment and killings into box office hits, mass exterminations into discussion panels, and unspeakable horrors into cash receipts. So, we flipped the pages of *Life* magazine to see what the latest celebrity was doing.

After all, all those terrible, unmentionable things, were "over there," in Europe and Africa, in Asia and South America. *We* were never bombed. *We* were never invaded. Our skies were never filled with war smoke, war ash, explosions. Our cities were never wiped out. Our family members' body parts were never scattered among the debris.

So, at the time, we tightened our belts, used our ration stamps, bought our bonds, and mourned our dead soldiers who died "over there." But in our land, we were free of the personal horrors of war and could never quite resonate with the wild language, metaphors, and desperate prose of our allies who walked stone-eyed and ash-dusted amidst the half houses and half bodies of their neighbors.

That is, until September 11, 2001. Then, the unbelievable happened. America was violated. America had been terrorized. In the very blue skies of a beautiful day there was sudden black smoke; and where there were two massive towers holding thousands of people—nothing. The halls of Congress were evacuated, leaders were led to bunkers, the Pentagon was smashed by an airplane and set afire, and airlines shut down. A continent of dismay and an ocean of tears flooded the land as people simply couldn't believe what they were seeing on TV.

Who among us will ever forget those images of the jets crashing into the towers, the fireballs of flame, the people jumping to their deaths from high windows, the towers themselves collapsing before our very eyes, the ash-covered streets, the herds of people walking zombie-like along the bridges, away from suffocating smoke, and the reports of brave people killed by falling concrete.

I remember one lady, a former parishioner of mine whom I hadn't seen in years, called to tell me that her son—her wonderful son—worked on the 100th floor of the Twin Towers. So many were no more and she was sick at heart, fearing that he also was no more. The people at the Armory, where they stacked bodies and what's left of them, asked her for his dental records and his comb to check the hairs for his DNA so they could compare them against body parts—not her son's intact body, but whatever bits and pieces they could find.

Then there were those people pitifully holding up photographs of their loved ones and walking around, pleading, "Have you seen my husband? Have you seen my daughter? Have you seen my father? Have you seen my niece? Have you seen my friend?"

And the chips fell unevenly. One person who worked at the Trade Center decided to take that day off to bring his son to preschool orientation. Years later, he was still badly shaken. On the other hand, another person's son just started work at the twin Towers and he's gone. Another, who worked on the eighth floor, above the fire line, escaped. Others below it did not.

Loud lamentations, worthy of the ancient prophets, filled the land as the country was brought to a standstill. It was like a bad movie come true and we're still reeling from its impact. Terror had arrived at our doorstep and we have not been the same since.

Today, we remember all of this as we find ourselves immersed in new horrors that leave us anxious and depressed: a global virus that has killed millions, the eruption of long-smoldering racism, a skyrocketing murder rate, anarchy in the streets, and a planet groaning with wildfires, typhoons, hurricanes, floods, and droughts. There is a shallowness of soul, a divided country, a deep wound in the body politic. Only 13 percent of Americans are satisfied with the way things are going in the United States.

A terrible scenario, and all I can say is that, with 9/11, we've been there before. We cling to the hope that, once we hit bottom, the individual heroisms and virtues of 9/11 will rise up again and coalesce, and the seeds of renewal will be sown. In short, the answer to our present catastrophes lies not so much in big programs, as important as they are, but in the small courtesies of life: the person who held the door open for you; the one who made you laugh; moments of grace; returning love for hatred, forgiveness for revenge; reaching out; being a moral person; writing the note; making the phone call; the thirst for justice; service to others; the forceful power of good deeds; personal integrity; the "I love you" said before it's too late; faith. In short, don't underestimate the cumulative force of small good deeds to someday turn our country around.

Let me end with a tale. A Native American grandfather shared this wisdom with his grandson. He told the grandson that we have two wolves inside us who struggle with each other. One is the wolf of peace, love, and kindness. The other is the wolf of fear, greed, and hatred.

"Which one will win, Grandfather?" the boy asked.

The wise man replied, "Whichever one you feed."

With our small acts of peace, love, and kindness, let us remember September 11 and begin to redeem each new September 11.

The land of the free and the home of the brave is worth it.[1]

---

1   A version of this reflection was previously published in Bausch, *Once Upon a Gospel*, 433–437, 37.

VARIOUS BLESSINGS

SENIOR GRACE BEFORE A CHRISTMAS MEAL

I give this blessing in the context of the old riddle: What did the lighted candle say to the darkness? Answer: the candle said, "I beg to differ."

Ours, in many ways, is a dark world, Lord: wars; ethnic cleansings; school shootings; broken relationships; a divided, soul-sick country; an exhausted climate; record rates of addiction, depression, and suicide among our young, as if they have given up hope.

But still—still, right now—we ask you to bless this season of gentle light, to bless the songs of our angels, the gladness of our shepherds, the guidance of the wise. Bless those who plant trees, tend to spiritual and physical sickness, open doors, take down walls, and build bridges.

We ask you to bless this joyous gathering: we, at life's limitations, grateful for this moment, pushing back the darkness with our feasting and laughter as we rejoice in the One who so loved the world that he gave us light to see by, light to live by, light to share by.

So, may kindness come with every gift and good desires with every greeting.

And, to quote theologian Howard Thurman,

When the song of the angels is stilled,
when the star in the sky is gone,
when the kings and princes are home,
when the shepherds are back with the flock,
the work of Christmas begins:
To find the lost,
to heal the broken,
to feed the hungry,

to release the prisoner,
to rebuild the nations,
to bring peace among [all peoples], to make
music in the heart.[1]

And I would add: to light candles, one at a time.

So, bless our food, we pray. Bless those who prepared it, bless those who are without it. Bless our festivity, our merriment, our togetherness. Finally, bless *our* light, dim or bright as the case may be—for that's all we have, but it is sufficient.

In your hands, it *is* sufficient. Amen.

A NON-TRADITIONAL BLESSING

May God bless you with *discontent* with easy answers, half-truths and superficial relationships so that you live from deep within your heart.

May God bless you with *anger* at injustice, oppression, abuse and exploitation of people so that you will work for justice, equality and peace.

May God bless you with *tears* to shed for those who suffer from pain, rejection, starvation and war so that you will reach out your hand to comfort them and to change their pain to joy.

May God bless you with *foolishness* to think you can make a difference in this world so that you will do the things which others tell you cannot be done.[2]

—Sr. Ruth Fox, OSB

· · · · · · · · · · · · · · · · · · · ·

1   Howard Thurman, "The Work of Christmas," *The Mood of Christmas & Other Celebrations* (Richmond, IN: Friends United Press, 1973), 23.

2   Ruth Fox, "A Non-traditional Blessing," as quoted in *The Almond Tree*, July 22, 2016, http://www.thesacredbraid.com/2016/07/22/a-non-traditional-blessing/.

A SIMPLE BLESSING

For use if you've been asked to give one at someone's birthday or similar event.

I've been asked to give a blessing before we eat but, in reality, I'm not here to *give* a blessing. I can't do that because blessing is already here, already present. Blessing is here in the person whom we honor today, precisely because *s/he* has been a blessing to so many of us, for so long.

I can't bless *her/him*—God has already done that. I can only focus on the fact that *s/he* is blessed. I can only reach back to *her/his* prototype, Mary, the mother of Jesus, who sang out then what *s/he* could readily sing out now:

> My soul proclaims the greatness of the Lord.
> My spirit rejoices in God my savior,
> for he has looked with favor on his
>   lowly servant.

> From this day all generations shall call me
>   blessed:
> The Almighty has done great things for me
> and holy is his name.

We, of several generations, do call *her/him* blessed today, and I can evoke that call.

So, as we prepare to dine, I extend, not a blessing, but a wish to *her/him* through an old folk ditty:

> May you always have work for your hands to do.
> May your pockets hold always a coin or two.
> May the sun shine bright on your windowpane.
> May the rainbow be certain to follow each rain.
> May the hands of a friend always be near you,
> and may God fill your heart with gladness to
>   cheer you.

And as for the food: May the Lord bless all here, and the food we are about to receive, through Christ our Lord, Amen.

APPENDIXES

APPENDICES

1. HOMILIES AND REFLECTIONS

ADVENT REFLECTION

A man dies. He had not, to be truthful, lived the worthiest of lives. In fact, he was something of a scoundrel, lying and cheating his way through life. Therefore, he found himself in hell after his departure from this life.

His friends, concerned about his sad—though well-deserved—fate, went down to hell and, moved by the man's misery, rattled those iron gates, calling out to whomever might be listening, "Let him out! Let him out!" Alas, their entreaties accomplished nothing. The great iron doors remained locked shut.

Distinguished dignitaries were summoned: powerful people, academics, intellectuals, prominent personalities. All of them stood at the gates of hell and put forth reasons why the man should be let out of this place of lonely torment. Some said that due process had not been followed in the man's eternal sentence. Others appealed to Satan's sense of fair play and compassion—as if he had any. They cried, "Let him out! Let him out!" but the great iron gates refused to budge.

In desperation, the man's pastor was summoned. The pastor came down to the gates of hell, fully vested as if he were to lead a Sunday service. "Let him out!" the pastor exclaimed. "He was not such a bad chap after all. Once, he contributed to the church building fund and twice he served meals at our soup kitchen for the homeless. Let him out!"

Still, the gates of hell stood fast.

Then, after all his friends and advocates had departed in dejection, the man's aged mother appeared at the gates of hell. She just stood there quietly, stooped and weak, crying. Finally, she whispered softly from the fullness of her maternal love, "Let me *in*! Let me *in*!"

And immediately the great gates of hell swung open and the condemned man was free.

And that, my friends, is Advent. Advent is a four-weeks cry of God, "Let me in! Let me into your human imprisonments, hopes, and fears. Let me into the burdens that crush you, the sadness of family members gone before you, or those whose bodies have fared well but whose minds have regressed. Let me into your illnesses and fractured relationships. Let me into your flesh and bones."

"Let me in!" God will plead for the four weeks of Advent. "Let me in to share, console, be with you, for my love is a mother's love, a father's concern, a brother's strength, a sister's healing. Let me in for Advent. Let me be the flesh that dwells among you, in you."

Somewhere in the north of Holland, there is a church where all those who entered used to bow down in the direction of a whitewashed part of the church wall before settling into the pews. Nobody knew why. They had been doing this from generation to generation, perhaps for a hundred or more years. Then, one day, the parish council decided to clean the walls. While doing this, they discovered some traces of a painting under the whitewash. Very carefully, they began to peel off the chalk, and they uncovered a centuries-old painting of Jesus on the cross.

Nobody remembered this picture. There was no record of it to be found. The painting had been lost from human memory. It must have been painted over centuries before, but the sign of respect had remained. That's a good metaphor for Christmas. People make vague gestures toward the manger, but they have whitewashed it with cuteness and sentimentality, and basically have forgotten what this feast is about, have obliterated the picture behind it. *Even good Christians have done this.* A recent poll found that the largest percentage of Christians interviewed said that Christmas was all about families getting together. Well, that's nice, but what about Christmas being about Jesus?

Even those who did mention Christmas as the birth of Christ, the origin of Christianity, tended to focus on the wrong things. They tended to focus on the emotion of it all: the appealing baby in the manger, the humble creche, the tableau of soft sweetness. Not one in a thousand, not one in a million—not even, I suspect, most of us here, would zone in on the one word—a rather shocking word—that the Bible, the Church, and Tradition tell us is really at the heart of Christmas. We too have forgotten.

That word we have forgotten is not sweetness, softness, or gentleness. No, it is *passion!* Does that surprise you? Yet, it's written all over the Christmas scene. The truth of the matter is that Christmas is not filled with sweetness, darlingness, and softness. We have here, this Christmas night, plain, unadulterated, hard, raw passion. I challenge you to recall that, yes, we have a cuddly baby, but behind that facade, behind that tenderness, is a fierce and a passionate God, and *that*—always—doesn't come across in the sentimental pageantry of the manger.

Take a second look. The Christmas message and the Christmas celebration center around God's great love for us, the commitment to not leave us abandoned, to not leave us in the darkness of political, social, or personal tyrannies. The message of Christmas is summed up in that communication the angel made to Mary at the Annunciation, "You shall call his name Jesus and he shall be known as Emmanuel, which translates, 'God with us.'" Yes, "God with us," or, in the reverential phrase of John's gospel, *Et Verbum Caro factum Est et Habitavit in Nobis:* And the Word was made flesh and dwelt among us.

Why? Why? Why does God want to dwell among us? *Because of desire.* Because, simply put, the object of *all* love is union: to be with the beloved. So, whatever it is, God has a thing for us—a Passion.

The real Christmas memory, then, is not that of a passive, seductive Baby Jesus, but rather of an active, *desiring God.* Christmas is about a driving desire on God's part "to dwell among us," to be a part of the human condition. God loves us that much. God yearns for us that much—and *that's* passion.

Maybe I can get my point across through a story, a story that mentions a baby. It's told by a woman, the baby's mother. Listen.

> It was Sunday, Christmas. Our family had spent a holiday in San Francisco with my husband's parents, but in order for us to be back at work on Monday, we found ourselves driving the 400 miles back home to Los Angeles on Christmas Day. We stopped for lunch in King City. The restaurant was nearly empty. We were the only family and ours were the only children.
>
> I heard Erik, my one-year-old, squeal with glee, "Hithere," the two words he always thought were one. "Hithere," and he pounded his fat baby hands—whack, whack, whack—on the metal highchair. His face was alive with excitement,

his eyes were wide, gums bared in a toothless grin. He wriggled and giggled, and then I saw the source of his merriment—and my eyes could not take it all in at once.

A tattered rag of a coat, obviously bought by someone else eons ago, dirty, greasy, and worn; baggy pants; spindly body; toes that poked out of would-be shoes; a shirt that had ring-around-the-collar all over; and a face like none other—gums as bare as Erik's. "Hi there, baby. Hi there, big boy, I see ya, Buster."

My husband and I exchanged a look that was a cross between, "What do we do?" and "Poor devil." Our meal came and the banging and the noise continued. Now, the old bum was shouting across the room, "Do you know patty cake? Atta boy. Do you know peek a-boo? Hey, look! He knows peek-a boo!"

Erik continued to laugh and answer, "Hithere." Every call was echoed. Nobody thought it was cute. The guy was a drunk and a disturbance. I was embarrassed. My husband, Dennis, was humiliated. Even our six-year-old asked, "Why is that old man talking so loud?"

Dennis went to pay the check, imploring me to get Erik and meet him in the parking lot. "Lord, just let me get out of here before he speaks to me or Erik," I thought, and I bolted for the door.

It soon was obvious that both the Lord and Erik had other plans. As I drew closer to the man, I turned my back, walking to sidestep him and any air that he might be breathing. As I did so, Erik, all the while with his eyes riveted to his best friend, leaned over my arm, reaching with both arms into a baby's pick-me-up position. In a split-second of balancing my baby and turning to counter his weight, I came eye-to-eye with the old man.

Erik was lunging for him, arms spread wide. The bum's eyes both asked and implored, "Would you let me hold your baby?" There was no need for me to answer since Erik propelled himself from my arms to the man. Suddenly, a very old man and a very young baby consummated their love relationship. Erik laid his tiny head upon the man's ragged shoulder. The man's eyes closed and I saw tears hover beneath the lashes. His aged hands, full of grime and pain and hard labor, gently, so gently, cradled my baby's bottom and stroked his back. I stood awestruck.

The old man rocked and cradled Erik in his arms for a moment, and then his eyes opened and set squarely on mine. He said in a firm, commanding voice, "You take care of this baby." And somehow I managed "I will" from a throat that contained a stone. He pried Erik from his chest, unwillingly, longingly, as though he was in pain.

I held my arms open to receive my baby, and again the gentleman addressed me: "God bless you, Ma'am. You've given me my Christmas gift." I said nothing more than a muttered, "Thanks." With Erik in my arms, I ran for the car. Dennis wondered why I was crying and holding Erik so tightly—and why I was saying, "My God, forgive me. Forgive me."

I would like to suggest that the real meaning of Christmas is in this story. Simply put, Erik is God. Simply put, the bum is us. Erik is God's yearning and passion for us tattered bums, with our tattered lives, our tattered hurts, our tattered relationships, and our tattered sins. Erik is two arms, determined to hug us. Erik is a fierce little baby who makes no distinctions but would embrace the least likely—you and me.

And the Word was made flesh and dwelt among us.

And *that's* what Christmas is about. It's an enormously unrelenting kind of a feast.

It is not sentimentality.

It is not soft.

It is not Sweet Baby Jesus.

Christmas is volatile Erik.

No, when you look at the manger, no cooing baby here. Only love satisfied.

This is why, when you come right down to it, we celebrate Christmas. If God is not with us and if God has not embraced our tattered lives, woe is us. There is no hope. And there is no light, only darkness and despair. And we are here tonight out of fruitless socializing, pressured routine, or empty sentimentality.

But if we are here because of love and we are here like the ragtag shepherds that we are, to humbly kneel and rejoice, then we have caught the meaning of Christmas: Emmanuel, the passionate God, has had his way and has hugged us fiercely.

A Merry, Passionate Christmas to you all![1]

· · · · · · · · · · · · · · · · ·

1   A version of this homily was previously published in William J. Bausch, *A World of Stories for Preachers and Teachers and All Who Love Stories that Move and Challenge* (Mystic, CT: Twenty-Third Publications, 1998), 458–462.

EPIPHANY: SLOUCHING
TOWARD BETHLEHEM

(Matthew 2:1–12)

T he gorgeous story of the Wise Men is among the favorites of Christian people. We love to hear it. We love to see the Wise Men's appearance at the crib with their royal clothes, elegant servants, and precious gifts. We love to point them out to our children and grandchildren. We love to weave romantic stories about them.

Gospel writer Matthew has indeed left us figures of high imagination. But, through all the traditions, can we make any educated guesses as to who they really were? Yes, there's a hint. Matthew says in his gospel that when Jesus was born, Wise Men came from the East to Jerusalem, asking, "Where is he who has been born the King of the Jews? We have seen his star in the East."

Now, although many translations are given—Magi, magicians, astrologers—it is very likely that these so-called wise men were priests of the Zoroastrian religion, who worshipped the god of light. They believed that every great person had a guiding light in heaven that appeared as a star—and the greater the person being born, the brighter the star. So, no wonder, when they saw this extraordinary star, they trekked across the desert in search of the one who must be very great indeed.

Their number? That has varied with imagination. Sometimes the number was given as twelve and sometimes the number was given as six. The six got entrenched for a long time because of confusion. In Milan, Italy, three relics of the Magi were supposedly honored. In 1164, there was an uprising and the relics were moved to Cologne, Germany. But, as time went by, people didn't know that bit of history and so they figured there were three relics in Italy and three in Germany, and that equals six Magi. Finally, however, imagination worked backward and figured that since there were *three gifts* mentioned—

gold, frankincense, and myrrh—the three gifts suggested three givers. Thus, our Zoroastrian priests of uncertain number have come down to us as the Three Wise Men.

But the impulse of storytelling could never let Matthew's tale rest there. In fact, it took a clue from Matthew himself by reaching back to the Old Testament. There, it found a psalm, the very responsorial Psalm 72 we used today, whose refrain states, "the Kings of Arabia will come bearing gifts." This psalm was applied to the Magi and so the three priests of Zoroaster were turned into Three Kings of the East. "We Three Kings of Orient Are" is our musical testimony to this development.

How about their names? In Matthew's version there are no names. Some would speculate that this was done on purpose and was consistent with Matthew's story. Since King Herod was running all over, killing anybody connected with the Christ Child, Matthew didn't want to use the names of the Magi since they and their descendants would thereby be in peril of their lives.

But, once more, imagination could not abide that lack for long and so, many decades after wicked Herod died, names were found. In fact, the names we have today were first found in some fabulous sixth-century mosaics in Ravenna, Italy: Balthazar, Melchior, and Gaspar. Even the gifts took on symbolism. Gold equals the virtue of these travelers. Frankincense, which is like incense going up to heaven, demonstrates how they were a people of prayer, daily lifting their voices to God. And myrrh, which is bitter and a kind of mineral, means they were willing to take on the bitterness and sacrifice necessary in their pursuit of the Holy One of Light.

Other stories and legends clustered around these very exotic people. One legend states that when they were over a hundred years old, they met again in the year 54 in Armenia to attend Midnight Mass, and then died shortly after. Another claims they went to India, where they were consecrated bishops by Thomas the Apostle, and they died in their dioceses.

Another legend, which is appealing, states that they were of three different ages. Gaspar was a very young man, Balthazar was in his middle age, and Melchior was an old man. When they arrived at Bethlehem, the three of them betook themselves into the cave of the Savior's birth, and they went in one at a time.

When Melchior, the old man, went into the cave first, there was no one there but a very old man his own age, with whom he was quickly at home, and they spoke together of memory and of gratitude. The middle-aged Balthazar encountered a middle-aged teacher when he went into the cave, and they talked passionately of leadership and responsibility. And when young Gaspar entered, he met a young prophet, and they spoke words of reform and promise.

Then, when they were all outside again after going in one by one, the three of them took up their gifts and went in together. And when they went in together, there was nobody there but a twelve-day-old infant. Later on, they understood—and so should we: The Savior speaks to every stage of life. The old hear the call to integrity and wisdom. The middle-aged hear the call to generativity and responsibility. And the young hear the call to identity and intimacy.

So, truly, the Three Wise Men have caught our imagination, and, when you think about it, noticeably more so than the other group in Matthew's Christmas story. There is, I think, a powerful reason for that.

That other group is the shepherds. Have you noticed that the shepherds have never really caught our imaginations and that we have few stories about them? The reason is that, in the gospels, the shepherds are told everything. They are encountered by an extremely talkative angel. This angel tells them every detail: where the Child is to be found, who is there, how to get there. When the shepherds arrive at the cave, the angel appears again to verify the place, and when the shepherds set out, they're guided by a whole heavenly choir of angels singing to them along the way. So, these shepherds have no doubts, no questions, no problems, no persecutors, no mystery. They didn't have to seek information. It was handed to them. They had it made.

That's not our experience. The easy-come, easy-go shepherds are not for us. Our experience is more likely that of the struggling Magi, for we, like them, are searchers. We have difficulty with the large questions of life. We too are harassed by modern Herods who seek to destroy our children with consumerism, pornography, materialism, and greed, offering them hedonism for heart, sensation for substance, celebrity for character.

And we worry and wonder about family life, AIDS, crime in the streets, illness, cancer, war, recession, pandemic, terrorism, and death. Yes, we too would like heavenly messengers and heavenly assurances, such as the shepherds got, but the fact is that we experience neither.

No, no doubt about it: It's the Magi, the struggling band crossing a hot desert with only a vision and hope to guide them, who resonate with us. They're our kind of people and we'll never tire of telling stories about them.

So, we'll stick with them, for the bottom line is this: The Magi didn't have all the answers, and neither do we. They had a wicked king after them. In many ways, so do we. But on their life's travels, what they did have was fellowship and the light of Christ to guide them, and so do we. But the best part of the wondrous Magi story comes at the end. For, at last, they found what they were looking for, and so shall we.[2]

. . . .

2   A version of this homily was previously published in Bausch, *Once Upon a Gospel*, 480–483.

ASH WEDNESDAY REFLECTION:
HOUSECLEANING

The origin of the word Lent is "lengthen" or, by association, springtime, when the days lengthen and spring housecleaning begins. Lent is a forty-day spiritual housecleaning. And, like with the house, it is needed. Despite our best intentions, we know that things have crept into our lives that are not of God, things that have to be cleaned out: the pettiness, the soft lies, the malicious gossip, the indifference to those in need, the "someday I'll do better" that never arrives, prayer that is rote and routine, a spiritual sloth that neglects nourishing the spiritual life, a coolness to God.

Just as, at housecleaning time, we move the furniture and find crumbs, dust, old papers, and all kinds of things, Lent is "moving the furniture" time. It's not just removing the dirt and sin, but also a matter of transformation, a realigning of our lives. Through prayer, works of mercy, almsgiving, and self-denial (perhaps replacing some TV time with spiritual reading), we begin to see things differently, to open up our hearts and minds to a fresh, deeper awareness of God within us and around us.

Note, therefore, that the ashes you are about to receive form a public notice to you and to the whole world: "Christian at work: Housecleaning in progress."

"*Jesus, knowing that the Father had given all things into his hands . . . got up from supper.*" So begins John's account. "All things into his hands"—from galaxies to grains of sand—and yet, he emptied those hands of such glories to take into them—our feet. Why? That he might wash them. Why? "Afterward, you will understand," he said.

Gradually, the Christian community *did* understand. It understood, when it reflected on whose feet they were and on the fact that Jesus resolutely did *not* look up. He did not look up because he didn't want to know the identity of the owners of those various pairs of feet, for his love was indiscriminate. He would not play favorites. He would wash all.

But he knew, as he began to wash. He knew that among those feet there were fishermen. He could tell. Their feet were rough, buffeted by nature and salt water. The feet of workers: the poor, the tired, the oppressed. Just like he remembered his father's feet when he was a little boy. Peter, James, and John belonged to those feet.

He knew he was washing honest feet. Perhaps he tried to guess which of the three owned them.

One of the pair of feet gave him pause, however. They seemed somehow . . . indecisive, not quite on the ground like the others. The kind that might give in to pressure? The kind whose owner would mouth a denial? No, maybe not. Still. . . . He paused a moment, and then went on to another pair of feet.

A zealot, surely. He guessed he must be at the feet of the zealot, Jude. The feet were not still. They were tapping on the earth: nervous feet, eager feet. Eager for reform, overthrow, perhaps a little terrorism thrown in. He washed them, hoping to reveal the man underneath the temper.

A doubter. Whose feet were these he was washing? The feet were pulled back, not pushed out front like the others. Someone hedging his bets? Someone not sure? Not sure of what? Jesus, the mission, the Kingdom? Concerned, Jesus moved to the next one.

Ah, obviously a tax collector. These were refined feet, used to sandals. Not burnt like the others. These feet had obviously spent a lot of time under the table where taxes were collected. And therefore—yes, therefore—an undesirable. A collaborator. An exploiter of his own people. A front for the enemy. "These feet need washing," he thought.

"Here's a simple soul. Soft feet, innocent, without guile. Must be Nathaniel's." Jesus paused and wondered, "Will Nathaniel be equal to the task ahead? Will he stay? Will he flee?"

Jesus moved to the final pair of feet. What's this? A *traitor*? One foot firmly planted in defiance, the other leading out ahead, like it's ready to bolt. Are these feet going somewhere tonight? Who *is* this? He washed these feet with extra tenderness.

"Do you understand what I have done?" he asked when he was finally finished and straightened up. Not really. The disciples did not understand at the time. As I said, it took time for the message to sink in. It took time to appreciate the love that was freely and equally given to sinner and saint—that, in fact, the Master would repeat this washing, this loving, time and time again, till time ran out.

For, one day, there would be a modern-day Peter, one with great power in the church; one, alas, with blindness in his heart to what was around him: the poverty, the injustice, the murders of innocent people. But, one quiet day, Jesus Christ took up his towel and basin once again and washed this prelate's feet and Archbishop Óscar Romero of El Salvador came out of the shadows to embrace his people and openly spoke out against an evil regime—and one day, standing at the Eucharist, he heard a rifle shot fired by that same evil regime, and he died at the altar, mingling his blood with the blood of Christ.

There was a zealot too: a woman of communist leanings and bohemian ways, with her live-in boyfriend and illegitimate child. But Jesus Christ stalked her and sought her out, and he washed her feet and took away her sins, and made this woman, Dorothy Day, hot for justice—this woman, this apostle of the poor, whose cause is now up for canonization.

This modern-day doubter was reluctant. Saucy and intellectual, too bright to believe, an unwed father, a gadfly of the books and colleges like Columbia University, which he attended. But, eventually, Jesus caught up with him, sat him down, and washed those feet with great love—and, like his namesake, Thomas Merton surrendered to it and became a convert, a monk, and a mystic.

This tax collector walked the corridors of power. He sat at the right hand of presidential power, and he connived and plotted and bled his own people. But Jesus patiently, slowly uncovered his feet and washed them, and Charles Colson, the most powerful man in the nation next to Richard Nixon, found himself in jail—and from there, a willing prisoner of the Lord who ministered in his name for the rest of his life.

This is one traitor who didn't get away. Oh, he denied everything, with his sharp wit and sophisticated pen. He mocked religion and laughed at the Catholic Church, and got others to laugh with him—that is, till *his* proud feet were washed by a humble Jesus and Malcolm Muggeridge—playboy, wit, editor of the famed *Punch* magazine—found himself a new man and an apostle for Christ, a convert to Catholicism.

That's what time has taught. What happened on that first Holy Thursday night, which we are commemorating, was a summary of Jesus' whole mission. Throughout the ages, he would love without condition and wash the feet of all—Peter's and Nathaniel's, Dorothy's and Thomas', yours and mine—without looking up; that is, without regard to position, prestige, or power; without regard to shame or sorrow or sin. All would be embraced, all would be cleansed, if we would but let him.

But there is one more thing. In case the message was still not clear, Jesus went on to make one final statement of his desire to cleanse us of our sins and remain among us as a servant. He took what was meant by the washing of the feet and found a way to remind us of it, to say it another way.

For, after he put down the towel and basin, he returned to the circle of disciples. There, he took bread and broke it, declaring it was his body "given for you." And then he took the cup and blessed it, declaring that it was his blood "shed for you." Different act, same message: Jesus serves. Jesus washes, Jesus forgives, and Jesus remains among us through the ages, ever ready to wash feet. The washing of the feet explains the Eucharist. The Eucharist explains the washing of the feet.

My friends, this is a holy night, awesome—full of awe. It bridges Passion Sunday and Easter Sunday and throws a light on them both. It offers us a challenge about the entire meaning of Holy Week.

Jesus asked then, and Jesus asks now, "Do you understand what I have done?" Do you? Do you understand such love, such humility, such desire? Are you willing to surrender to it?

You have your chance. We are now going to wash the feet of the disciples. I ask you to imagine your face on each one's face. Put your feet into each person's feet, and therefore into Jesus' hands, and tell him, confess to him, how much you need cleansing. And then, renewed, when it comes time, you will be able to receive the Body of Christ that "has been given for you." And you will understand.

My son Bobby got sick last week," says this father. "I took his temperature, and it was 102.5. Out came the children's Advil. He slugged down a dose, and 15 minutes later his fever was back down to 100. Just before bed, I checked his temperature again. It was back up. More Advil. I checked again 45 minutes later; now it was 103. By midnight, his skin was hot, he was lethargic, and his temperature was 104. I called the hospital. 'Bring him in as soon as possible,' they said. I told him we were going to the doctor. Bobby looked at me with weary, wondering eyes and asked, 'Am I going to die, Daddy?' Immediately, I had three reactions. Common sense: 'No, you are not going to die. We just need to get this fever down.' Emotional: 'I'm scared.' Visions of children with bizarre diseases flooded my heart. Spiritual: 'Dear Jesus, cover him. Heal him. Love him.'

"'No, Son, you're not going to die,' I told him. I didn't want to scare him. I was fairly certain his fever was not life-threatening. But my mind flashed to the many parents in this world who have had to look at their children, knowing that the ultimate answer to that question is 'yes.' And I wonder if, in the heavenly places, there was once a conversation between the Father and the Son, when the Son asked the question, 'Am I going to die, Daddy?' and in his heart, the Father knew the answer was, 'Yes.'"

My friends, we have just finished a week—Holy Week, we call it—in which that "yes" was worked out in a sad and sickening way: the betrayal on Wednesday; the agony on Thursday; the horrific, brutal death on Friday; the stillness and grieving on Saturday. But then, the burdened body, carrying our weight, rose anew on Sunday, the day we call Easter, the moment that has brought us here today in all of our finery because we are spiritually rejoicing over the opportunity for the newness of life, and grateful that, because of Jesus who "bore our infirmities," death no longer is the final word. *This* is gospel, Good News, indeed, and "Alleluia!" is the only response.

This we acknowledge. But, in the long run, for the mind, these are often mere words, familiar words that have perhaps lost their power from that very fact, words we know and casually recite in our creed. But it takes more than the head to sense the love, the very deep love, that is evident in the Son's yes. It takes the heart. It takes the heart to be moved to embrace the love that took on our burdens and redeemed them. So, we need a symbol, a powerful image to make us both weep and rejoice in gratitude—and make us remember.

Here is the image, embedded in a story. Listen with your imagination, with your Easter heart.

Way before the dawn one Friday morning, I noticed a young man, handsome and strong, walking down the alleys of our city. He was pulling an old cart filled with clothes, both bright and new, and he was calling in a clear, tenor voice, "Rags! Rags! New rags for old! I'll take your tired rags!"

"Now, this is a wonder," I thought to myself, for the man stood six-feet-four, and his arms were like tree limbs, hard and muscular, and his eyes flashed with intelligence. Could he find no better job than this, to be a ragman in the inner city? I followed him—my curiosity drove me—and I wasn't disappointed. Soon, the Ragman saw a woman sitting on her back porch. She was sobbing into a handkerchief, sighing and shedding a thousand tears. Her knees and elbows made a sad X. Her shoulders shook. Her heart was breaking.

The Ragman stopped his cart. Quietly, he walked to the woman, stepping around the tin cans, dead toys, and used Pampers. "Give me your rag," he said, so gently, "and I'll give you another." He slipped the handkerchief from her eyes. She looked up and he laid across her palm a linen cloth so clean and new that it shone. She blinked from the gift to look at the Giver. Then, as he began to pull his cart again, the Ragman did a strange thing. He put her stained handkerchief to his own face and then *he* began to weep, to sob as grievously as she had done, his shoulders shaking. Yet she was left without a tear.

"This is a wonder," I breathed to myself, and I followed the sobbing Ragman like a child who cannot turn away from a mystery.

"Rags! Rags! New rags for old!"

In a little while, when the sky showed gray behind the roof tops, the Ragman came upon a girl whose head was wrapped in a bandage, whose eyes were empty. Blood soaked her bandage. A single line of blood ran down her cheek. Now, the Ragman looked upon this child with pity, and he drew a lovely yellow bonnet from his cart.

"Give me your rags," he said, tracing his own line on her cheek, "and I'll give you mine." The child could only gaze at him while he loosened the bandage, removed it, and tied it to his own head. The bonnet he set on hers, and I gasped at what I saw, for with the bandage went the wound! Against his brow ran a darker, more substantial blood—his own!

"Rags! Rags! I take old rags!" cried the sobbing, bleeding, strong, intelligent Ragman. The Ragman seemed more and more now to hurry.

"Are you going to work?" he asked a man who leaned against a telephone pole. The man shook his head. The Ragman pressed him. "Do you have a job?" "Are you crazy?" sneered the other. He pulled away from the pole, revealing the right sleeve of his jacket—flat, the empty cuff stuffed into the pocket. He had no arm.

"So," said the Ragman, "Give me your jacket and I'll give you mine." Such quiet authority in his voice! The one-armed man took off his jacket. So did the Ragman—and I trembled at what I saw, for the Ragman's arm stayed in the sleeve, and when the other put it on, he had two good arms, thick as tree limbs, but the Ragman had only one. "Go to work," he said.

After that he found a drunkard, lying unconscious beneath an army blanket, an old man, hunched, wizened, and sick. He took the blanket and wrapped it round himself, but for the drunk he left new clothes.

And now I had to run to keep up with the Ragman. Though he was weeping uncontrollably and bleeding freely at the forehead, pulling his cart with one arm and stumbling for drunkenness, falling again and again, exhausted, old, and sick—yet he went with terrible speed. On spider's legs, he skittered through the alleys of the city, this mile and the next, until he came to its limits and then he rushed beyond. I wept to see the change in this man. I hurt to see his sorrow. And yet I needed to see where he was going in such haste, perhaps even to discover what drove him so.

The little old Ragman—he finally came to a landfill. He came to the garbage pits. And then I wanted to help him in what he did, but I hung back, hiding. He climbed a hill. With tormented labor, he cleared a little space on that hill. Then he sighed. He lay down. He pillowed his head on a handkerchief and a jacket. He covered his bones with an army blanket. And then he died.

Oh, how I cried to witness that death! I slumped in a junked car and wailed and mourned as one who has no hope, because I had come to love the Ragman. I sobbed myself to sleep.

I did not know—how could I know?—that I slept through Friday night and Saturday and its night too. But then, on Sunday, I was awakened by a violent light. Light—pure, hard, demanding light—slammed against my sleeping face, and I blinked and I looked, and I saw the last and first wonder of all. There was the Ragman, folding the blanket most carefully, a scar on his forehead, but alive! And, besides that, so healthy! There was no sign of sorrow, nor of age, and all the rags he had gathered shone in their cleanliness.

Well, I lowered my head and, trembling for all that I had seen, I got out of the junk car and walked to the Ragman. I told him my name with shame, for I was a sorry figure next to him. Then I stripped myself of everything and I said to him, with yearning in my voice, "Dress me. Make me new again!"

He dressed me, my Lord did. He put new rags on me, and I am a wonder beside him.

Thus, in parable, is the story of this week: We have traveled from the burdened Ragman to the Risen Christ. From "Crucify him!" to "Alleluia!" From fear of death to hope of resurrection.

It's been a great triumph for divine love. No small wonder that we can wish each other, "Happy Easter."[3]

· · · · · · · · · · · · · · · · · ·

3 A version of this homily was previously published in Bausch, *A World of Stories*, 101–103.

n the Passion narrative this past week, we heard this episode. Jesus was with his disciples in the Garden of Gethsemane on the Mount of Olives. While he was speaking to them, Judas arrived with a large armed crowd. He went up to Jesus and kissed him, the prearranged signal to the soldiers, saying, "Greetings, Rabbi." And Jesus asked, "Friend, why are you here?"

Today, I have the same question. Friends, why are you here? This, after all, is the Catholic Church of the media headlines, the devious and corrupt church, the church branded with a large scarlet letter that besmirches the gospel, tarnishes good priests, and shames Catholics everywhere. So, friends, why are you here?

Beyond your own private responses, let me suggest an answer. We are here because of what I call the Easter Church, the bedrock church.

By that I mean the everyday church, the church that continues to display quiet, persistent, daily heroism outside the radar of the media. For over 2,000 years, ordinary people have done deeds of love, forgiveness, charity, and compassion in the name of the Risen Savior. Among them are the people who taught us how to read and write and preserved civilization during the dark ages, and the people who founded and, to this day, operate the hundreds of thousands of schools, leprosaria, hospitals, orphanages, and the largest AIDS support network in the world. People in our history include a deacon, Francis of Assisi; a wife and widow, Catherine of Siena; a soldier named Ignatius of Loyola; and an archbishop from San Salvador, Óscar Romero, whose assassination was ordered by the controlling powers because he spoke out against their oppression of the peasants.

Closer to home, there is our contemporary, convert Dorothy Day of Staten Island, who founded the Catholic Worker Movement and whose cause is up for canonization, not because she once was a communist, a common-law wife, or had an abortion, but because she discovered in our Easter

Church the Risen Jesus and showed a heroic and profound concern for the poor.

Then there are the 19 million people who entered the church doors on Easter in 2012. That's 2,169 every hour, or 36 every second. There are the millions upon millions who went to Mass every weekend, the massive crowds who came on Ash Wednesday and Palm Sunday, Christmas and Easter.

There is the Easter Church of Catholic Relief Services, the largest single private charitable organization in the world, given the highest marks by secular committees because almost all of its collected money goes to direct care.

I could go on, but listen to columnist Nicholas Kristof, whose *New York Times* Op Ed piece sums it up. He wrote:

> In my travels around the world, I encounter two Catholic Churches. One is the rigid all-male Vatican hierarchy that seems out of touch. . . . Yet, there's another Catholic Church as well, one I admire intensely. This is the grassroots Catholic Church that does far more good in the world than it ever gets credit for.
>
> This is the church that supports extraordinary aid organizations like Catholic Relief Services and Caritas, saving lives every day, and that operates superb schools that provide needy children an escalator out of poverty. This is the church of the nuns and priests [and lay people] in the Congo, toiling in obscurity to feed and educate children. This is the church of the Brazilian priest fighting [disease]. . . . This is the church of the Maryknoll Sisters in Central America and the Cabrini Sisters in Africa [who risk their lives] in Swaziland to visit AIDS orphans. . . .
>
> So when you read about the scandals, remember that the Vatican is not the same as the Catholic Church. Ordinary lepers, prostitutes and slum-dwellers may never see a cardinal, but they daily encounter a truly noble Catholic Church in

the form of priests, nuns and lay workers toiling to make a difference.[4]

To these words, let me piggyback an excerpt making the blog rounds. It's from a man named Sam Miller, a prominent Cleveland Jewish businessman. He writes:

> Why would newspapers carry on a vendetta on one of the most important institutions that we have today in the United States, namely the Catholic Church? Do you know—the Catholic Church educates 2.6 million students everyday at the cost to your Church of 10 billion dollars, and a savings on the other hand to the American taxpayer of 18 billion dollars? Your graduates go on to graduate studies at the rate of 92%. . . . The Church has 230 colleges and universities in the U.S. with an enrollment of 700,000 students. The Catholic Church has a non-profit hospital system of 637 hospitals, which account for hospital treatment of 1 out of every 5 people—not just Catholics—in the United States today.[5]

Now, if all that doesn't suggest why you are here, let me end by taking you to the movies.

As some of you may know, a powerful movie, filmed in Morocco, has been made about that country. The name of the film is *Of Gods and Men*. It won the Best Foreign Language Film of the Year, the Grand Prix in 2010 at Cannes, and the Lumière Award for Best Film.

It's the true story of seven Roman Catholic Trappist monks at Our Lady of Atlas Monastery in Algeria during the Algerian Civil War in the 1990s. Their mission as monks—who are lay people, remember—is to live a life of prayer and contemplation

. . . .

4   Nicholas Kristof, "For a Church Mary can Love," *The New York Times*, April 20, 2010, https://www.tampabay.com/archive/2010/04/20/for-a-church-mary-can-love/.

5   Sam Miller, as quoted in John F. O'Brien, "Be Proud to be Catholic," *Cleveland. com*, updated March 28, 2019, https://www.cleveland.com/ireland/2008/08/be_proud_to_be_a_catholic.html.

and, in addition, to serve the wretchedly poor people in the area by giving them medical assistance, comfort, counseling, and education. It's a dangerous place where they live. Islamic terrorism is at every corner and grows more intense each day. The monks are increasingly witnessing with horror the ruthless murders of the townspeople. They have heard about the murder of European construction workers by terrorists and recoil on hearing about the stabbing by Islamic fundamentalists of a woman riding on a bus because she was not wearing a veil.

They begin to realize that they cannot long escape the same fate if they remain there. In fact, the Algerian government has asked the monks to leave for their own safety. Ominously, it's not long before a group of fundamentalists shows up at the monastery, on Christmas Eve, demanding medicine for their wounded colleagues. Though their request is refused—the monks need the medicine for the desperate people—the Abbot quotes the Koran to their leader and they end up shaking hands, but the Abbot knows in his heart that they will be back.

And each monk also knows that, sooner or later, when the fundamentalists *do* come back, they will have to decide what to do: to flee or to stay. Ultimately, in a most poignant scene, the movie takes us, the audience, into the monks' chapter room, where they candidly struggle to come to a decision that has to be unanimous. Shall they flee to safety or shall they stay, with the understanding that they will most certainly be killed? Their discussions are long, measured, respectful, and quiet, with stretches of profound silence. We, the audience, are allowed to gaze into their searching eyes as each one lays bare his fears, his struggles, his ambiguity, his faith, his soul.

Finally, compassion and humility win out and the monks decide to be the Easter Church, to stay where they are and not abandon the people. They feel deeply that Jesus, who had sent them there to work and pray among the oppressed people of Algeria, would not want them to abandon their work, no matter the danger, or the suffering. The monks, in effect, have decided to offer the world the possibility of another way to live and to die, of what the world might look like transformed by grace.

Then, the high point of the film arrives when the monks recreate the Last Supper by sitting around a small table, drinking wine and listening to a recording of Tchaikovsky's *Swan Lake*. As the camera pans from face to face, we observe a beatific smile on some faces, tears on others, apprehension on all. This is it.

Not long after their "Last Supper," in 2005, they were all beheaded. As he approached his death, the Abbot, obviously mindful of Jesus on Calvary, addresses the unknown Islamic militant whose sword would kill him: "You, my friend, who do not know what you are doing—yes, for you too, I give you farewell and commend you to the God whose face I see in yours." Then his head rolled into the dust.

These monks were imitating Jesus, who gave his life for others.

Friends, why are you here? I think you are here because of those monks—because, whatever your journey, whatever your misgivings, whatever your doubts, whatever your faithful or unfaithful observances, whatever the faults of the Church in the headlines, you somehow intuitively recognize the persistent presence of the Risen Jesus in this Easter Church, where there is still the same bread, the same wine, the same teaching, the same scripture, the same gospel, the same baptism, the same forgiveness, the same outreach, the same healing, the same quiet heroes, the same faith, hope, and love—all in the name of the One who was risen 2,000 years ago and is with us today.

Yes, the felt presence of this Jesus is here in this Easter Church of ours. Mock him, beat him, disfigure him—and, Lord knows, we've done it all—he remains. His words and his works remain. His church remains. He is here, and that's why I am here, and perhaps, deep down, you also.

Have a blessed, hopeful Easter.[6]

---

6   A version of this homily was previously published in Bausch, *The Story Revealed*, 66–70.

PENTECOST: THE HOLY SPIRIT AND PAPA GOD

Priests have always been targets, not just in times of persecution because they were leaders—think of the thousands of Polish priests who died at Auschwitz under the Nazi terror—but in benign times. Because the Roman collar and black suit mark out the priest, kids stare at him and slightly tipsy women at wedding receptions, glass in hand, weave their way over to him and ask to have their confessions heard. The men remark with knowing looks that, now that Father's here, they'll have to watch their language and off-color jokes, and the hosts see that he is seated with safe people. Priests don't mind. It's a minor misery. They expect that. It goes with the territory. But they brace themselves for the inevitable angry bore—not infrequently an ex-Catholic—who spots the collar from across the room and makes a beeline for his target. "Why in the hell are you wasting your time in that stupid church? I finally wised up and got out."

Then, obviously having read Dan Brown, Richard Dawkins, and Christopher Hitchens, he goes on to spout the familiar litany of all that is wrong with religion in general and the Catholic Church in particular: the Inquisition, the Crusades, the bad popes, sinister bishops, Vatican conspiracies, clerical sex scandals, the degradation of women, dull Masses, lousy sermons, money-grubbing clerics, and so on.

Of course, I am familiar with that litany of accusations. The church has had, and does have, many problems, and too often is like a dysfunctional family. So, why stay? Why put up with such misery? Why? Because of Jesus' words in today's gospel: "I will give you another Advocate to be with you always." *Always*, notice.

This always-abiding Presence, this Holy Spirit of Pentecost, makes the difference. *That's* why we put up with it. Jesus promised to be with us, no matter what we may be like on any given day: when we're good and when we're bad, when we're heroic and when we're cowardly, when we're faithful and when we're not.

Now, you can choose to believe or not to believe in this presence of the Holy Spirit. If you choose not to believe, you can check-list the church's problems and walk away in disgust. You can believe the church is nothing but a pack of barking dogs baying at a silly monkey atop a tree. But, if you choose to believe, then you must look not only for signs of church failures, but also for signs of the life-giving Spirit.

Then you will begin to notice how, with great regularity, in the worst of times, in the depths of misery, God has a tendency, out of nowhere, to raise up holy ones who advertise the presence of the Holy Spirit. A Catherine in the kitchen, a Charles de Foucauld in the desert, a Damien in the leper colony, a Mother Teresa in the slums, a Thomas Merton in the Village, a reformed alcoholic priest in the debris of 9/11.

Pentecost, friends, celebrates that. It celebrates the abiding presence of Jesus, the persistence and surprises of the Spirit that give us reasons to remain Catholic.

This truth calls for reinforcement, so I have a parable for you. It's a folktale from Haiti. As you listen, I ask you to think about Pentecost.

Once upon a time, in the middle of a great forest, there lived an old woman who kept hives of bees. By the end of the summer, she had more honey than she could use: every jar, bowl, and barrel were filled to overflowing with the sweet golden honey. The old woman kept some for herself. The rest she poured into a great pot, lifted the pot on top of her head, and set off to market. Off she went through the great forest for days with the pot balanced on her head.

But, just as she neared the marketplace, she accidentally caught her foot on a tree root and went flying. There was a great crash. The pot had fallen and smashed to the ground, oozing the sweet, sticky honey all over the forest floor. The woman just sat there and began to cry.

"Oh misery!" she moaned, "Papa God, you send me too much misery!" After a long while, she finally got up and trudged home with a heavy heart, crying all the while, "Misery! Oh misery! Papa God, you send me too much misery!"

Now, it so happened that a little monkey, sitting high among the branches, saw the whole thing. As soon as the woman was out of sight, he swung down to the ground. He looked and looked at the strange sticky stuff. He had never seen anything like it before. Cautiously, he dipped one of his fingers into it and touched his lips.

"Oh, my," he exclaimed to himself, "this misery is good! I've never tried misery before." He scooped up a whole handful and swallowed it. He ate and ate until he got down to licking the pot, persisting until there simply wasn't any more. Oh, but there had to be more. "I want more!" he cried.

And then he remembered overhearing the old woman saying, "Papa God, why'd you send me so much misery?" He scratched his head. So that's where misery came from! "Maybe," he thought to himself, "maybe if I paid Papa God a visit, he'd give me some more misery." And the more he thought about it, the better the idea seemed.

So, off he went. Back to the trees and then to the mountains, he climbed and climbed until at last he came to Papa God's house. And there was Papa God himself, sitting in the garden, just watching the world.

"Beg your pardon, Papa God," he shouted.

Papa God turned and saw him and smiled. "Ah, little monkey, what do you want?"

"Begging your pardon, Papa God," said the little monkey, "more than anything else, I want misery."

Papa God looked puzzled. "You want misery, little one?"

"Oh yes, sweet, sticky misery. I want as much as you can give me, Papa God."

Papa God got up, thought a minute, and said, "Well, it just so happens that I have got some special misery made just for monkeys. Are you sure you want it?" The monkey nodded his head.

So, Papa God went inside his house and, after a spell, returned carrying a leather bag. He said to the monkey, "Little monkey, this bag is full of misery. Now, you must pay attention and do exactly what I tell you. First of all, you must carry this bag to the middle of a great sandy desert where there are no trees and where, in fact, they can't grow. Then, once you're there, you will slowly open the bag and inside you'll find more misery than you ever dreamed of."

The monkey was delighted and wasted no time. He took the leather bag and climbed back down to the world and he ran and ran until he came to the edge of a great desert and then he ran and ran some more until he came to its very center. Exhausted, he sat down. His hands were trembling in anticipation of all that misery.

So, he opened the drawstrings of the bag just as Papa God had told him, and out came real monkey misery—DOGS! One, two, three, four, five, six, and seven huge, hungry black dogs!

The monkey screamed, dropped the bag, and literally ran for his life. The seven black dogs were snapping at his tail. They were getting closer and closer. And just when he thought he could go no farther and the dogs were sure to get him—a tree appeared!

Out of nowhere, a huge, great tree appeared, right there in the middle of the desert, where trees, of course, do not grow at all. The monkey scampered up the tree as fast as he could, leaving the seven snarling dogs leaping up and down at the trunk.

For the rest of the day, he sat in the tree branches, quaking with fear, until the sun went down and the dogs, frustrated, eventually slunk away. As soon as they were gone and the monkey thought it was safe, he climbed down and ran for the forest as fast as he could, and never looked back.

Now, the question—the Pentecostal question—is this: Where did that tree come from? Who put that great tree where trees don't grow, right there in the middle of a hot, dry desert? I'll tell you. Papa God put it there. Why? Because Papa God knows that too much misery is not a good thing, even for a monkey.

The message is this: We rejoice in the mercies and put up with the miseries of our church because we believe with all our hearts that, true to Jesus' promise, the always-present Spirit continues to grow trees where they don't grow.[7]

· · · · · · · · · · · · · · · · · ·

7   A version of this homily was previously published in Bausch, *Once Upon a Gospel*, 145–148.

2. RESOURCES

One of the side effects of being isolated is that people have time to read. Most of us turn to murder mysteries or novels or catch up on a favorite interest: history, science, literature, popular magazines, and so on. That's well and good. Still, with time on one's hands, it is also an opportunity to refresh or catch up on religious subjects. If our reading is totally secular, or indiscriminate TV watching, addictive and larded as it is with vulgarities and millions of consumerist commercials, our spirits will shrivel and our horizons narrow until we miss any signs of God's presence.

This is not an academic book, so I don't want to take up space and time except to remind you that isolation is a good time to deepen your faith and learn more about it. There are excellent resources out there, resources not only for personal growth but also for communal interaction via Zoom and other such platforms. I must warn you that, unfortunately, like our polarized country, Catholics run the gamut, from the extreme right to the extreme left, so you have to be careful to tap into balanced resources. Seek the advice of balanced people. Some suggestions:

1. Subscribe to your diocesan paper.

2. Subscribe to a good Catholic magazine. There are the mainstream ones like *Catholic Digest, Ligourian, St. Anthony Messenger Press, Catholic Update, Commonweal* (liberal), *First Things* (conservative), and many more.

3. Be in contact with your local parish for references.

4. Read anything by William J. O'Malley, SJ. His *Daily Prayers for Busy People* (Liguori, 1990), *Lenten Prayers for Busy People* (Orbis, 2004), and *You'll Never Be Younger: A Good News Spirituality for Those Over 60* (Orbis, 2015) are gems, the last one right up our alley.

5. There is a great *Shorter Christian Prayer* (Large Type Edition) that contains the official liturgy of the hours (divine office) that the monks and priests pray morning and evening (Catholic Book Publishing, 2004).

6. Join a Catholic Book Club or read one of those four-page updates you probably receive regularly.

7. Online: The secular media is not favorable to religion in general and Catholicism in particular, so, to get a truthful and well-rounded view, subscribe online to CRUX. It's an essential: https://cruxnow.com/.

As for other online resources, there are many choices. Probably the overall best is from Bishop Robert Barron, with his multi-faceted offerings for liturgy, books, devotions, Mass, teaching, current events, and so on. Contact him at https://www.wordonfire.org/.

Finally, the pandemic has forced the local Church to reach out in creative ways. Many Catholics watched Mass on TV or by streaming from their local parishes. Moreover, they learned that they could surf the internet for the most interesting and compelling preachers or teachers, and for news and online courses. That was the upside. The downside is that they could discover qualities they do not find at their local parishes and may wind up preferring the more interesting online Catholicism rather than what they find in their local communities. And that would be a loss, not the least of which is the loss of Communion, the Eucharist being the heart and soul of Catholicism. My guess is that the future Church will be a hybrid of personal and electronic contact. It will take time to come to some kind of a balance.

O.K. time to end this manual with Tennyson's famous words:

Though much is taken, much abides; and though

We are not now that strength which in old days

Moved earth and heaven, that which we are, we are,

One equal temper of heroic hearts,

Made weak by time and fate, but strong in will

To strive, to seek, to find, and not to yield.[1]

- - - - - - - - - - - - - - - - - -

1   Alfred Lord Tennyson, *Ulysses*.

Made in the USA
Middletown, DE
24 December 2021

56781834R00126